Bart!

Bart!

THE

unauthorized

LIFE & TIMES

ins AND *outs*

UPS AND

DOWNS

O F

Lionel
Bart

b y

DAVID
ROPER

PAVILION

FOR MY FATHER AND FOR MY MOTHER

First published in Great Britain in 1994 by
PAVILION BOOKS LIMITED
26 Upper Ground, London SE1 9PD

Text copyright © David Roper 1994

Designed by Nigel Partridge

The moral right of the author has been asserted

A CIP catalogue record for this book is available from the British Library

ISBN 1 85793 330 3

Typeset in Bembo 11½/15 pt

Printed and bound in Great Britain by Hartnolls Limited, Bodmin, Cornwall

2 4 6 8 10 9 7 5 3 1

This book may be ordered by post direct from the publisher.
Please contact the Marketing Department.
But try your bookshop first.

The author and publishers are grateful to the following for permission to reproduce
illustrations: Associated Press Ltd: nos. 11, 12; Cavalcade Pictures: no. 6; Zoe Dominic: no.
16; Jack Grossman: nos. 1, 2; Lumiere Pictures Ltd: no. 14; The Raymond Mander & Joe
Mitchenson Theatre Collection Ltd: nos. 8, 15, 17; Mirror Syndication International: no.
20; The Robert Opie Collection: no. 7; Pictorial Press Ltd: nos. 3, 4, 13; Popperfoto: nos.
9, 10, 18, 21; Solo Syndication: no. 19.

And to the following copyright holders for permission to quote copyright material:
Bloomsbury Publishing: from *Alma Cogan* by Gordon Burn, p.viii; Daily Mirror:
'Whatever Happened to Lionel Bart', pp. 107–8; Harper Collins: from *The Kenneth
Williams Diaries* edited by Russell Davies, p. 9; Lemon Tree Press: from *Why Fings Went
West* by Frank Norman, pp. 26–7; Lion Publishing: from *Cliff Richard* by Steve Turner,
pp. 20, 167; London International Books: from *From Drags to Riches* by Danny La Rue,
p. 10; Methuen London: from *Joan's Book* by Joan Littlewood, p. 27, and from *The
Dynamics of Creation* by Anthony Storr c/o Peters Fraser & Dunlop, p. 149; Macmillan
London Ltd: from *East End, West End* by Bernard Delfont/Barry Turner, pp. 87–8.

Every reasonable effort has been made to acknowledge the ownership of copyrighted
material included in this volume. Any errors that may have occurred are inadvertent, and
will be corrected in subsequent editions provided notification is sent to the publisher.

CONTENTS

ACKNOWLEDGEMENTS

Thanks will never be adequate to honour the debt owed to Al Senter for his meticulous additional research and assiduous interviewing skills. They will, however, suffice for Nicholas de Jongh, the benefit of whose experience has not been overlooked. And, let us not omit Tinu Majekodunmi for her unquestioning loyalty, Nick St George for his patience and, for their unfailing memories: Cliff Richard, Anthony Newley, Leslie Bricusse, Ned Sherrin, John Gorman, Jack Grossman, John Gold, Mark Bramble, Ed Wilson, Brian Lee, Tim Mellors, Derek Block, Johnny Speight, Brian Kirk, Robert Farrant, Victor Spinetti, Peter Wilson and the many who prefer to remain unnamed.

Any account of a life – whether one's own or that of another – is necessarily partial, selective and imperfect. This has not been an easy book to write: it began as a project to co-author Lionel's autobiography. As with others who had tried before me, Bart eventually tired of the exhaustive process required to produce a substantial documentary work, and called it off. Sadly, Lionel's memory is unreliable: good anecdotes are made better over the years by the retelling of them, and some have reached a point where they are irreconcilably parted from the truth. Because this book had to be completed to a very tight schedule, many of Lionel's innumerable acquaintances and former colleagues will have been overlooked – or rather, placed on the list of those the author would like to contact, should this book have a subsequent revised edition. To those who may feel their account should be more widely heard, I urge them to contact me through the publishers.

Throughout the research period, Lionel, with understandable justification, asked his four or five closest friends to withhold their participation. Most complied out of a sense of loyalty. And yet, it is clear that, had this been an authorized account of Lionel's life, he would have issued the same injunctions about many aspects of his past with which he feels uncomfortable. However, if Lionel or they would like to make any future contribution, their experiences would be valued.

The atmosphere – scuzzy sex and booming hangovers and complex interpersonal dynamics – brought back memories, as it always does (as I look forward to it doing), of all those mornings when the tour bus was loading up to head off for another town in that period in the mid-to-late fifties, roughly between *Blackboard Jungle* and Little Richard finding God and dumping his jewels in the Tallahassee, when the world seemed to be being made new and new energy was flowing into all departments of everyday life.

In 1957, the business was still coming off that big beautiful sound of Patti Page and Perry Como and Kay Starr. That was fading away and the new sound was taking over.

FROM *ALMA COGAN*
BY GORDON BURN

'It's very strange to be haunted by your past. Your songs are still being played, you're a clue in a crossword puzzle or you're mentioned on TV panel shows. Strange...'

LIONEL BART, 1986

OLIVER! OLIVER!

Lionel Bart woke up on the morning of his thirtieth birthday to discover that he was famous. It was 1 August 1960. Everyone wanted to know him. Everyone wanted to give him hospitality. It was a very strange feeling. And yet, it was inevitable...or so the newspapers had been telling him.

The West End was undeniably hungry for it: hungry for a show that would break a run of seventeen flops in seven months, and hungry for a truly British musical to rival the success of *Oklahoma!* or *My Fair Lady.* It had been six years since *The Boy Friend,* and although Bart's *Fings Ain't Wot They Used t'Be* was still running, it seemed as though the Roaring Sixties, as the *Record Mirror* was calling them until they started Swinging, were waiting for Lionel and *Oliver!* to ignite the fuse.

Lionel Bart had become 'our very own Irving Berlin', the 'Prince of Denmark Street' and the 'Golden Boy of Tin Pan Alley' and any number of other superlatives that hacks want to shower on what they see as overnight success. He had only been in the business for four years, but undeniably had no trouble composing a hit song – and no trouble doing it in about sixty minutes sitting in one of his luxury cars with a portable recorder. And how the press adored the trimmings: the four cars, including a Facel Vega (number four, with the registration plate 45 WPE, bought with the proceeds from *Oliver!* and each car with its own telephone – as rare as hen's teeth in the late fifties); the flat in South Kensington; the entourage of Rank starlets. It was what the sixties were supposed to be: some of us had really never had it so good.

Oliver! had its first night on 30 June 1960. Lionel took his seat in row twelve of the stalls. The opening number launches the action, as there is no overture in *Oliver!* The show starts with the workhouse kids queuing up for their daily bowl in a rapturous chorus of 'Food, Glorious Food'. In the next scene the beadle and his wife capture rebellious little Oliver, who dared to ask for more, and put him into a cell. Then safely on to Scene Two, a little domestic encounter between Bumble and the widow at the workhouse, and a song called 'I Shall Scream'. At this point, one of the twin revolves is supposed to come forward a short way to establish the interior. But the revolve does not move as far as it is meant to – perhaps less than a foot. The audience does not know. Only the actors, the director and the designer are aware of the incident. And, of course, Lionel.

Immediately, it presaged doom and disaster to the anxious creator. And that was enough to cue his swift departure from the premises. Under cover of the darkness, he raised himself to a stoop, eased his seat up, and fled quietly into St Martin's Lane. It was a glorious summer evening, and Bart needed a walk to calm himself down. First, down to Trafalgar Square, where he did a complete circuit of Nelson's Column, then up Haymarket to Piccadilly Circus to visit what might almost be deemed his patron saint – Eros.

It was perhaps an hour and three quarters before he came back down St Martin's Lane. As he approached the New Theatre, a threatening rumbling noise leaked from its four sets of glass swing doors. The nearer he walked, the more ominous it became: the sound of a mob – a mass chant, like a Ban-the-Bomb cry. It was a sound Bart dreaded, the noise of discontent he had anticipated the moment he escaped two hours earlier. As he was to admit later: 'I was terrified. I had convinced myself that they thought it was bloody awful.' And at that moment, Donald

Albery, the owner, manoeuvred himself on his one good leg out of the theatre and up to the composer, saying, 'You've got to go in.' With the help of a commissionaire and a few ushers, Bart was hustled through the stage door and straight into the wings to an absolute commotion.

The entire company was on the stage. What Bart did not know was that they had taken as many as twenty-three curtain calls. They had sung all the reprises of 'Consider Yourself'. The house lights were up throughout the auditorium and the entire audience was standing in spontaneous, genuine tribute. As Bart was flung on to the stage, the cry went up: 'Speech. Speech. Author!' It was the cry he had heard while lurking outside in the street.

Lionel Bart's mother was in the audience for the première of *Oliver!*, seated somewhere in the dress circle. His first gesture was to thank her from the stage. Then, with equal chivalry, he thanked Charles Dickens with 'May the Good Dickens forgive us' (some were later to suggest that it should have been a more abject apology, though that was not the mood on this occasion); at which a voice from the gallery riposted: 'You've done a wonderful job.' And at that minute the band started up again, the company all reprised 'Consider Yourself', but still the audience refused to leave, and in the end the entire stalls – or as many of them as could – climbed up on to the stage. In Bart's own words: 'It was quite ahead of its day. I've never seen that happen before or since, except when they did it in *Hair*, but that was part of the planned ending. It just went on and on, and I don't remember too much more about that night because it was just loads of faces – joyous faces is all I can remember.'

Of course, West End first nights at that time were still very much black-tie affairs, and some even clung to the notion that they should be nothing less than top-hat affairs. There was certainly no shortage of glamour that evening at the New Theatre. Rex Harrison turned up – to the delight of the emergent breed of paparazzi. He had been in the country only a few hours, after eight months in the States. Bart's dearest friend Alma Cogan came, Max Bygraves, Jess Conrad, Judy Carne and, on Lionel's arm, the 'film starlet' (as the reporters would have it) Jackie Lane.

No one can remember where it went on to, or even if it went on.

There was no organized party, since nobody had expected anything like that overwhelming reception. There were surely a few drinks on the stage, though Lionel claims there was no drunken blackout.

And it was from that moment that this tyro musical genius knew that there was no need to worry about the notices: word-of-mouth would see the show all right. Which is not to say that some critics weren't going to be gloatingly hostile to the success of someone, not just of his age, but who had had the audacity (unheard of since the Master, Noël Coward) to write book, lyrics and music. And (unlike the Master) without being able to read a single note.

Lionel Bart did not wait up for the newspaper reviews to be rushed from Fleet Street that night. He woke up the next morning in bed at Reece Mews, where the staff brought all the morning papers in to him. The phone never stopped. 'I guess I realized then that I'd made my niche somewhere, and it probably began to dawn on me that I was famous.'

CHAPTER ONE

MUMS AND DADS

I s there really anything left unsaid about the East End of London during the inter-war years? It's all there in the constantly rediscovered Bert Hardy photographs from *Picture Post*, in the grainy film footage of John Grierson, the scratchy recordings of 'My Old Dutch'. As with the Gorbals, the documentary evidence of the gor-blimey-me-ol'-sparrer Cockney community has turned itself into the reality. There is now no violence, there are no bottle gangs, no health or sanitation problems, no unemployment. These have all been replaced by glowing, heartwarming nostalgia – barrer-boys who'd never say anything more challenging than 'Gawd bless ya', hopscotch played on the chalked-out squares of the scrubbed pavements bordering glistening cobbled streets, friendly (if snotty-nosed) children with nothing more sinister on their mind than how far they could travel behind a hoop and stick.

Into this monochrome, Movietone world, in what was known as Mother Levy's maternity home at 24 Underwood Road, E1,[1] on 1 August 1930, Lionel Bart was born. It might not have been. She was, after all, forty-six when she gave birth to this, her last child. She had already given birth ten times before.

Yetta Darumstundler had married Morris[2] Begleiter in 1910 in their native Galicia, which was then part of the Austrian Empire. 'They fled to England during a pogrom, but my father was not allowed in, and was held on the Isle of Man for the duration of World War I. So my mother arrived in London with her mother, then eighty-four years old, one daughter and another child on the way. She had to bring up the kids and look after Grandma with no income and no profession. Thankfully, there were people from her village living in the East End, and those were the days when everybody looked after everybody else.' They were also the days when housing conditions were often pitiable, when two-thirds of all householders paid rent (sometimes as much as a third of their incomes) to private landlords for overcrowded accommodation without running water.

As much as 35 per cent of the population at that time was living more than two to a room, and 15 per cent more than three to a room. Almost half the families in Shoreditch, Finsbury and Islington shared their homes, often with two or three families to a house. In Stepney, as late as 1931, the census reveals that over 50,000 people were living two or more to a room.[3] And yet, Bart recalls that no one ever went hungry, since no one was ever overlooked or abandoned. It was not only a community, it was an extended family and, for the Jewish immigrants, a community within a community.

Of Yetta Begleiter's eleven children, seven survived. 'There was an interval of six years between my big sister Renee and me. I was the last, an afterthought. Mum was forty-six, and Dad was well into his fifties when I was born. I was always known as the Baby and fussed over a lot. Sometimes I was neglected, being the youngest. Other times, I was loved to distraction.' Dad was by now established with a workshop at the back of their house at 43 Ellen Street, just off Cable Street in Whitechapel, as a master tailor, a profession adopted by every member of the family – except the youngest. It would be facile to suppose that this rebellion was born of resentment at being that unwanted burden, the 'runt of the litter' Bart believed himself to be. Yet it would be as dishonest not to recognize the source of some of his constant cravings for admiration...and affection. Lionel himself acknowledges that many of his later problems had their origins in those days of self-doubt. In compensation, he persuaded himself that he was 'special', and lived with the conviction that one day the world would share his belief that fame was his due. 'I was interested in dressing up, showing off, and I wanted to be the leader of the gang...and I became the leader of the street gang. I was very fast on my feet. You had to be fast or funny when you were little. And I was little. I was also good with lyrics at an early age, good at making up rude words to current popular songs. I was Mr Smartypants. My earliest ambition was to be famous. For what, I did not know. I just wanted to be unique, and recognized for it.' No more, perhaps, than any youngest infant needing to establish a character strong enough to outshine those of his siblings.

Even Lionel's parents were moved to consider the child some kind of prodigy when, on his thirtieth birthday, they looked back from the splendour of their new flat (deposit of £600 paid by Lionel), with its modern green furniture (bought by Lionel) and its fresh flowers (sent by Lionel) in Stamford Hill, London, N16. Mrs Begleiter considered her riches, and claimed she had always had faith in her son's ability and determination to succeed beyond his appointed measure. 'A very good boy. Our seventh child, God bless him. He's not snobbish like some boys who make money and forget their parents. We're just ordinary, working-class Austrian refugees. Without Lionel, we couldn't have done all this on our old-age pension.' His father, by now in his eighties, believed it was when Lionel was six that they discovered his leanings. 'My wife went to see his headmistress,' he explained. 'She said he was an artistic genius, so I paid for him to have violin lessons, like I always wanted. He also learned to play the piano with one finger, then with four fingers. Just enough, you know, to help him with his songs.' Just enough, and no more. It is one of Lionel's boasts that he has never had to play more than that in order to write some of the twentieth century's most popular tunes. Dad bought the boy his own violin for £2 from one of the stalls in Petticoat Lane, close to where they lived at the time. 'After six months, all I could play was "The Bluebells of Scotland". The music teacher told my father he couldn't bear to listen to me any more.'

In 1990 Bart told an interviewer: 'I remember my dad telling me, "Li, all I want is for you to be a mensch." A mensch is Yiddish for a real person. A real person: that's all he ever wanted me to be. And it's taken me all this time to find out what he meant.' But just what did the patriarch mean? Bart has an equally strong memory of his father, one he has never made public, and not one to inspire his confidence or self-esteem. His father had taken him to the public baths for a swim, and started to make fun of the boy in the changing-room with jokes about the size of his penis – quite likely, the seemingly innocuous joke any father occasionally makes; although Lionel remembers his father asking whether, in fact, Lionel hadn't been born a girl, in view of how small his 'willy' was...If Lionel, by the age of sixty-four, has exorcized the deep scar this made on him, he clearly had not when as a teenager he was called to his National Service medical: 'I can remember his words, and they stopped me from being able to pee into the specimen bottle when the examining doctor asked me to. It was so humiliating...something I'll never forget.'

And in case anyone misses that connection between the poverty, the pain and the persecution on the one hand, and the fruitful cradle of Jewish artistic talent on the other, the roll-call contemporaneous with Lionel Bart's own entry included the names Wolf Mankowitz, Arnold Wesker, Harold Pinter. Just as his parents had learned to tolerate the blind prejudice of the Great War, when their accent led people to think they were German and thus could not be included in any commercial or social intercourse, so Bart learned in childhood that, being a Jew, he would have to brave the usual bigotry on his way up from the bottom of the East End entertainment melting pot. Unlike, say, the Grades or Frankie Vaughan, Lionel for a long while carried an inborn caution and awareness on matters of race or social conscience. He had a theory on why so many musical shows were written by the Gershwins, the Berlins, the Hammersteins – fellow Jews.

'I feel that all life is a search for love...a desire to be loved. And nobody is more guilty of this vice, of needing to be approved of, than minority groups like Jews. That is why they make such brilliant entertainers. That is why they go into showbusiness. That approval and that applause...it's a kind of love, isn't it? People like me, who came from the gutters of the East End, we haven't got time for all that surface chi-chi.

We have seen too much that is true and real. Look at Wesker. All that guts and reality, man! Look at Pinter. You know what it is? It's a search for truth. That's what it is.'

Perhaps, borrowing Proust's metaphor, Lionel could also have mentioned that other exclusive club to which membership is always granted, never requested. Lionel also had a desire to be loved. Not continuously, but continually. Not consistently, but constantly. Like the 'alternative' musical contingent that numbered among its membership Noël Coward and Ivor Novello, Lionel found himself a double outcast. He knew from childhood that he would be his father's son in the line that stretched back to Abraham and Moses. But he would never be his father's mensch. Never introduce his mother to 'the right girl'. In 1940s Britain, such 'unnatural and unspeakable' tastes were only ever mentioned in music-hall jokes. They were reserved for cravat-wearing members of the theatrical classes. And, possibly, that was an underlying attraction of the theatre to anyone who needed to have access to like-minded artistic admirers of Sparta. As Kenneth Williams reveals frequently in his diaries: 'In the past, it was always enough just to say that I felt I belonged to the world of the theatre. Certainly this still applies, for I can think of no other sphere into which I can fit ideally.'[4] If it was an arena for flamboyance, it was also one devoid of prejudice, except from without. In 1952, under the headline 'EVIL MEN', the *Sunday Pictorial* broke the conspiracy of silence to tell its readers what they might not have known, but in all probability had widely suspected, about 'pansies' in the simplest and most informative of statements: 'homosexuality is rife in the theatrical profession'. What, after all, could be lower than a pantomime pansy, less savoury than a backstage bum-boy? The dressing-room was the last refuge of the hounded – a private place with private codes, special manners, even a rarefied language of gay polari[5] that caused no raised eyebrows. To the world outside, the longer this seething pit of weak wrists remained behind locked stage doors, the safer and cleaner that better world would be. In a discussion on the Wolfenden Report, proposing law reforms to decriminalize homosexuality, the *Daily Telegraph* reassured its readers: 'homosexuality in any form, if legalized, may spread like an infection. Medical opinion is divided, but to the lay mind it seems clear that the law should provide against the possibility.'

Could it be that Bart's first physical fumblings on the outskirts of this night-time underworld came during the Second World War? As a ten-year-old, he was evacuated from London in 1940 in anticipation of air raids over the capital, but he himself has often talked about his illicit return visits – the unwanted jinx who always brought in his wake a scorching Blitz on his East End streets. His contemporary, Daniel Carroll,[6] also evacuated, remembers the Luftwaffe squadrons making their first sorties over Docklands in September 1940, and the Londoners' well-rehearsed routine of registering at the air-raid shelters in deep basements or Underground stations, where families were allocated their own section for the night. 'I was amazed by the sheer volume of people inside the shelter. Masses of men, women and children were huddled together in sleeping bags, on top of mattresses and bunk beds, and under blankets, in what resembled a huge subterranean barracks room. People from every walk of life were thrown together in times of adversity. They coped extremely well. In a very short space of time...friendships were forged and the refugees from the Blitz banded together in camaraderie and brotherhood to share whatever fate had in store for them.'

In all likelihood, Bart was as familiar as Kenneth was with pubs like the Salisbury, near the New Theatre in St Martin's Lane, or the Bear and Star, opposite Wyndham's Theatre in Charing Cross Road, which Danny describes as 'a pub where artistes of all kinds would congregate and spend the time of day together. When the pub closed, we moved on to the Express Dairy for tea and sandwiches, and to discuss how good or bad we all were.' Such places bred circumspection, rather than openness, however, and it was ten years before this kind of sexual behaviour was commonly discussed. Two days before the opening of *Oliver!* the *Daily Mirror* of 28 June 1960 summed up the debate for legalizing behaviour that had accepted being driven underground: 'Many people understandably still feel uneasy about relaxing the law...Yet it is sometimes the duty of Parliament to act ahead of public opinion. This is one of the times. Homosexual conduct is a private sin, like adultery. However odious, it is a matter of conscience. The law should no longer be called upon to punish it as a crime.'

The change in the law came too late for Bart, Williams and others of their generation – not morally too late, nor physically too late: mentally, they were unable to change. They had learned and subconsciously accepted a way of living in two worlds – visible to the one, invisible in the other: secrecy, furtiveness, slyness...When, in July 1967, the Lords passed Leo Abse's Bill, legalizing in England (but not in Scotland, Northern Ireland or in the services) the sexual act between two consenting males over twenty-one in private, it was too late to shed this cloak of self-deception, a modus operandi that had worked until then, and would have to continue to work if they were not to reinvent themselves in a further confusing act of voluntary schizophrenia. And who can be surprised, when the *Daily Express* heralded the law reform with the vanquished squeal of vacuous self-righteousness in these words of 12 July 1967: 'What benefit can this proposed legislation bring to anyone – least of all to the unfortunate men most directly affected? Unnatural practices will become more easily indulged. A social stigma will be weakened...Parliament only brings discredit on itself when it separates itself so decisively from the moral will of the people.'

Moral education aside, Bart's interrupted wartime schooling continued in peacetime with a scholarship to St Martin's School of Art, then in London's Charing Cross Road, where his first life model was Quentin Crisp. Records for 1946 (he left the following year) show the commercial art student L. Begleiter, aged sixteen, having won a scholarship for a place on a course which should have turned him out as a certificated printer, graphic designer or sign-writer. But, according to Lionel, he was expelled from the institution three or four times for being mischievous. Art schools are, after all, also on the fringes of society, and known to foster 'liberal' behaviour, as David Hockney's memoirs of beatnik days at the Royal College of Art reveal. Added to which, St Martin's was on the fringes of Soho with its newly opened coffee bars welcoming home young war heroes and lingering Americans with their new relaxed attitudes to prevailing moralities. It was Bart's father who, once again encouraging him to do 'different' things from the rest of the family, had sent the boy to learn a trade in design. Bart did quite well while he was there: 'But I gave up the idea of becoming a painter because painters always work alone, and I like a good mob working around me.' Nevertheless, Lionel was evidently proud of the canvases he created, some of which formed part of an exhibition of mostly pregnant women ('I was attracted by the look in their eyes and their all-over glow') and kept many of them at home. It remains a deep wound within him that, returning from his two-year absence in the forces, he discovered that his mother had taken the art works from the basement where they were stored, and mistakenly gave them all to the dustmen

When his National Service requirement came up in 1948, he applied to the RAF and, despite his difficulties with micturition at the medical, was accepted as a clerk. The only plane he ever saw was a vintage Spitfire embedded in concrete at the station gates.[7] 'I never did anything apart from painting a mural in the NAAFI and editing the station magazine. One of the chaps I met in the RAF had been a printer, and he and I decided we didn't want to work for anybody when we came out. After I was released, I took jobs around the coffee bars for a while. Then I borrowed £50, and John Gorman, this chap I'd met in the RAF, and I started a printing business in a Hackney basement.' The company was founded in 1950. By 1960 the business was employing forty-three people, and continues today as G & B Arts, run by Gorman's son, though Bart is no longer a partner, having resigned in the mid-1960s. Bart's relationship with John Gorman took them both into the Communist Party and, that membership aside, has surprisingly endured. Gorman was the man called to pick up the pieces when Bart's life was shattered thirty years after that first meeting.

His other lasting relationship, forged in the early 1950s, also endures almost without interruption to this day. Lionel often recalls how his sister Renee[8] was addicted to theatre and music-hall, but was never allowed to visit either without her brother as chaperone, and from these enforced trips sprang his love of drama. John Gold[9] provides a no less prosaic account. 'I first met Lionel around 1950 at the International Youth Centre, which was a club for people in their twenties of left-wing views, and there would be a dance on Saturday nights by Chelsea Embankment, advertised in the *New Statesman*. During one dance, Lionel and I put on a little cabaret with a few others that was very well received – so much so that they became a regular attraction. In 1952 Lionel and I got together to write the annual IYC Revue, and I remember one sketch about Robin Hood, as written by Dostoevsky and Noël Coward, which may well have been the forerunner of *Twang!!*

'I'd say that Lionel was sympathetic to the aims of the IYC, but he was never overtly political. I can recall him as a very vivacious person, bursting with zest and life and Jewish charm. I was attracted by that vivacity and extraordinary creativity – he was like a firework exploding in all directions all the time. What's more, he was a very rapid worker, his mind seemed to race ahead creatively. Anyway, we were so encouraged by the success of the IYC Revue 1952 that we both went along to the Unity Theatre to audition for the production of Leonard Irwin's *The Wages of Eve*.'

After work, Lionel and John spent their evenings in Goldington Street, near King's Cross Station, where the left-wing amateur group Unity Theatre had its base. Unity had been founded in 1936 and, in addition to being the first company in this country to stage Brecht, had established the 'living newspaper' technique with a documentary on the London bus-strike of 1938. One of the first productions Bart worked on was a play about equal pay for women, called *The Wages of Eve* – a Romeo and Juliet love story across the picket-line of an industrial dispute in which the young trade union leader finds the charms of the boss's daughter dangerously irresistible. Lionel understudied the lead role. 'There was a notice-board at the theatre, and a notice went up to ask if anyone was interested in writing some songs, so I did a couple for a laugh. I sang the songs to someone who could write notation, pinned them on the notice-board, and forgot about them really. I just carried on painting scenery until Alfie Bass[10] collared me and said he thought they weren't half bad.' The song-words, as they were known then in the theatre, were for a tune called 'Turn It Up' and surfaced in the political revue of the same name, which was directed by Bass. John Gold remembers Lionel winning admiration for his talent and antagonism for his bulldozing approach to fellow workers in the theatre. Despite that, Bart's lyrics were regularly commissioned and used, and survive in Unity's

13

agit-prop version of *Cinderella*, which the London *Evening News* decided was 'just as the kiddies in Moscow would understand and adore it'.

Among his contemporaries was Jack Grossman, today a writer and documentary film-maker, who has a clear memory of Bart's involvement. 'Unity encouraged people to do everything – act, write, paint the scenery – we all mucked in. Anyway, a call went out for people to contribute to a revue. It was to be a satirical political revue – Unity was doing this kind of show long before *That Was the Week That Was* – and Lionel and I kind of gravitated towards each other. I remember going to his house in Stamford Hill, and meeting his parents. Lionel had a piano upstairs – he was always known as the 'one-finger merchant' – and we'd sit and kick ideas around. Some of us would agonize for days about writing, but Li always had a tremendous facility. You thought up a theme, and he would come back the next day with ten lyrics...eight crap, but two terrific. I don't think Lionel was at all political. He didn't appear to share the left-wing views the rest of us held, but he had a great talent for picking a headline in the newspaper, extracting its essence, and making a song of it.

'The revue became *Turn It Up* and Lionel and I wrote several numbers, including "Coronation Mugs" – it was 1953, after all. We then went on to write *Cinderella* together for the following Christmas, and Li played Lavinia, one of the Ugly Sisters. I remember vividly the day of the Dress Rehearsal when he came on in full drag with a plunging neckline revealing his hairy chest! They made him cover up with a net after that. Lionel was always very dedicated...whatever he did, he was never late, never missed a cue, and he was always the first to arrive in the dressing-room. Conditions were very spartan and very cramped, but he always managed to find himself a corner, and woe betide anybody who encroached on his space.

'A lot of people used Unity as a stepping-stone to other things, and Lionel and I were no exceptions. I always knew he would fit into whatever surroundings he chose...he's a bit of a chameleon and he's always been a good bluffer. He never did have that sardonic detachment with which we saw the showbiz world...he loved rubbing shoulders with famous people. You could say he was very much in the spirit of the times: here was a working-class boy taking advantage of the fact that there were no longer any social rules. Nobody said you can't do that or don't go there...cometh the hour, cometh the man.'

Doubtless fired by unanticipated encouragement, and perhaps fostered also by the Unity's resident dramatist Ted Willis,[11] Bart contributed to another revue, *Peacemeal*, and was accepted in the company as a writer, now doing less scenery-painting, understudying and poster-designing, in order to improve his dramaturgical talents. In the *Record Mirror* of 1958, 'twenty-six-year-old Lionel Bart' (he was, in fact, within a fortnight of being twenty-eight at the time) was credited with having written his first musical. It was called *Wally Pone, King of the Underworld* and established a Cockney theme that has run through almost all Bart's subsequent stage work and not a few of his pop songs. An updating of Ben Jonson's Jacobean comedy of manners about a successful con-man who is finally unmasked by those he dupes, it was scheduled for a London try-out at the Unity from 18 July, and ran for a respectable eight weeks. And in *Encounter* Colin MacInnes was admiring Bart for possessing 'a certain English essence of sentiment and wit'.[12]

There remains one other significant amendment to his life. This took place in 1951 – or rather, the event did not take place: Lionel made a decision, and engineered the event. The twenty-one-year-old East Ender with a passion for amateur dramatics embraced existentialism, and began seriously to map out his destiny. It was his name: it would not do. Alfie Bass had the right ring to it – plain, simple, memorable. Lionel Begleiter did not. And this was also an opportunity to give himself some class, to secure – even illicitly – admission to the circle which had at its centre his hero Noël Coward. Ask Bart how he chanced upon his new identity, and he will deliver a story perfected by years of telling and re-telling. He was on a bus passing the London hospital St Bartholomew's, when the name took his fancy. And yet no record can be found of Lionel Begleiter[13] ever having made an official application to change his name by Deed Poll to Lionel Bart. Moreover, what he could not have foreseen was that, like himself, this new chosen name would pass into Cockney lore in its turn. 'Phew, who's dropped a Lionel?' is an easy clue to the unsavoury, and certainly unclassy, meaning behind the abbreviated rhyming slang.

CHAPTER TWO

CONSIDER YOURSELF

L ionel Bart had a head start on Philip Larkin when it came to sexual intercourse. At least a full decade. The youth of the 1950s was learning fast: in 1954, the charts were in thrall to Doris Day's two new releases 'I Speak to the Stars' and 'Secret Love'. Tony Brent was Columbia's golden hope with his version of 'Three Coins in the Fountain'. Bryan Johnson's programme *Melodies Old and New* on Radio Luxembourg was showcasing Alma Cogan for a full fifteen minutes in July, leading to a *Record Mirror* encomium that began, 'Alma Cogan improves with every performance. The vitality, personality and pep positively exudes from this talented young lady who has now definitely established herself as one of Britain's top-notch singing stars.' Yet it was a perch she had to share with Anne Shelton, Donald Peers, Ronnie Carroll, David Whitfield, Dickie Valentine, Edmund Hockridge and Ronnie Hilton, storming the hit parade in 1956 with 'No Other Love'.

Other likes, though, were emerging. Archer Street, part of the Tin Pan Alley area, was described as knee-deep in marijuana joints. Artistes were being encouraged to try a new wonder-drug called methylpentynol, guaranteed to stop the shakes in a recording session...with no noticeable side-effects. Then, in the same year Mel Torme released 'Mountain Greenery', a catchy number called 'Rock Island Line' leapfrogged straight to number three. The youth of 1956 may have been callow enough to consider Lonnie Donegan the epitome of suave sexuality, but his personal significance to a generation that had not yet become 'teenagers' was smaller than the significance of skiffle music with its washboards and tea-chest basses. What mattered about skiffle and its improvised bands, was where the music was heard. Milk bars and coffee bars, serving frothy brews in transparent Pyrex cups on matching saucers, sprang up in a Britain that had been starved of fun for what seemed like always. Post-war austerity had been the country's blue period. Now the blues gave way to a new mood, one of youthful confidence and over-confidence, plus the chance to be young without disapproving looks from parents. Whether it was from work or from the Welfare State, the young also had enough buying power to demand their own entertainment, whether live, on disc, on celluloid or – later in the decade – on television. As soon as the word 'teen-ager' (coined in that form by Frankie Lymon's backing group) was heard, it brought with it associations of leisure, pleasure and conspicuous consumption. And, as often as not, it was partnered by the worship of motorcycles (scooter-riders not yet being the sworn enemy), by Friday nights in dance halls, by smoky jazz clubs, by Melody Bars, by the sharp suits of teddy boys, by a hip, coded language that changed its argot daily, and always by 'jungle music' – the most audible witness to the end of the civilized order an earlier generation had fought for to the death in a recently won war. To these old daddios, rock 'n' roll was several notches down the evolutionary scale even from skiffle, and its attraction was as incomprehensible as that of the duffel-coat or the Gaggia machine.

The press carried reports from America of switch-blade fights and arbitrary destruction, after which Bill Haley would invariably comment, 'You can't blame the music.' In the music press, commentators viewed the new bastard's arrival from a sceptical step back. Not wanting to lose their loyal jazz, latin or popular readers, the reaction was: 'Rock and Roll. No ducking it, this shrieking, stamping, misbegotten offspring of "rhythm and blues" remains a top controversial topic.' One more opinionated critic came right out with it, calling rock 'n' roll 'a token symbol of the inferiority complexes and sundry aberrations of certain puerile groups'. Liberace was on a month-long tour, *Oklahoma!* was top of the album charts (just ahead of *Rock Around the Clock*) so why should the editor of the *Record Mirror* be hasty? Instead, he preferred to ask: 'Will there be too many Rock 'n' Roll shows on the variety halls – or not enough? Isn't this problem worrying certain booking agents who, despite initial successes with R 'n' R, just can't gauge how long the craze will last?'

Rock was a world exclusive to youth; it was the raw roar of a momentary, carefree hedonism. And, as such, it needed its own self-replenishing supply of heroes, who had to be as maltreated and misunderstood as those who came to worship them. It also needed its shrines, where such sacrifices and sacraments could be enjoyed without scandalizing the non-believers. South London had a number of premises known as SPO-joints. The letters stood for Sausages, Potatoes and Onions, and these three indivisible elements of basic nutrition wallowed greasily throughout the day on enormous enamel platters in the windows of the establishment, waiting to be slopped up before anyone who had sufficient appetite to withstand the gastric dangers. One of these 'joints' was located near the railway arches running beneath Waterloo East Station. To meet the needs of local youngsters it upgraded itself into a club called the Cave, concealed behind a well-known yellow door. It was here that Bart first met a blond, doe-eyed teenager from Bermondsey with a white-toothed grin called Thomas Hicks, who recalls their first encounter. 'We'd been invited to go to a party at a place called the Yellow Door. We were told that it was off The Cut, which is a small street with the Old Vic on the corner. And in the middle of this bombed ruin, nicely lit by gaslight, was a yellow door, and there were all these beatniks inside...and one of them was Lionel. And me, Lionel Bart and Mike Pratt[1] came away from there that night, and over the next six or seven months we formed a group, and called ourselves the Cavemen, because that's what was on the other side of this yellow door. And we wrote a song called "Rock With the Caveman", which was a spoof...it wasn't meant to be a pop song. And that was the beginning of three careers.'

The year was 1956. And, just as Lionel had adopted the surname of a local hospital, so nineteen-year-old Tom from Bermondsey wanted the world of screaming girls to know him as Tommy Steele. His rise from the mess-deck of the Cunard Line (where he was a bell-boy) to guest TV appearances and top of the bill at the Finsbury Empire took less than eight weeks. On leave from his ship, Tommy had asked at the 2 I's coffee bar whether he could play guitar and sing during a session, without pay. Johnny Kennedy, then still a gimmick-conscious publicist and house photographer for the *Record Mirror*, spotted the talent, and in partnership with Larry Parnes,[2] a refugee from the rag trade with a stud farm of bankable lads, booked their irresistibly lovable confection into the Stork Club. When, a fortnight later, Tommy passed his Decca record audition, they rushed out the Bart–Pratt–Steele song 'Rock With the Caveman', which was at number three in the hit parade by November. On the proceeds Bart, Pratt and two other friends bought an old London cab for £12, shipped it across to Scandinavia, and bummed their way around Europe for a few weeks.

The mystic formula Bart–Pratt–Steele (sometimes the order would be different, though doubtless merely for variety) began to appear on the incomprehensible slips of paper which circulated in the catalogue departments of record companies. These were known as 'label copy', and were typewritten versions of what, with luck, would finally be printed on the labels of the records themselves. Bart played washboard as well as playing around with the lyrics: 'Rock With the Caveman' contains some unlikely five-syllable words and excruciatingly banal rhymes.

Still, as Bart already knew, the medium was not the message. 'The kids couldn't have understood it, but they all sang it.' His stint on the washboard with the Cavemen lasted only a matter of months. Lionel was no musician, and the Cavemen were soon reorganized as the Steelmen, leaving him free to concentrate on his songwriting.

The 2 I's coffee bar in Soho's Old Compton Street[3] became the mecca for dedicated followers of fashion who were too young to gain lawful entry to public houses and too old to hang around church youth clubs. And it owed part of its sudden appeal, and part of its décor, to Lionel. On 14 July 1956, a young commercial artist called Wally Whyton asked whether he and his skiffle group the Vipers might be allowed to play in the dank basement beneath the espresso bar. 'Paul Lincoln said it was OK, and within about three weeks the place was literally packed to the doors. Instead of letting us busk, he charged a shilling admission and paid us two pounds a night each. The basement had been a store room and, when we became the resident group down there, I went with Lionel Bart and a couple of others and painted designs on the walls.'[4]

Even before Tommy had reached the age of majority, Bart and Pratt were being asked to write enough rock 'n' roll songs to fill a film biography of the singing sensation's brief existence. 1956 was the year some cinemas in Britain had been brave enough to screen a film produced by Sam Katzman, featuring a chubby, quiffed rocker in a satin DJ. The movie was *Rock Around the Clock*, and was followed the same year by the same team with *Don't Knock the Rock*. But Bill Haley was not alone in being the voice of a generation. Elvis released *Love Me Tender,* and then *Jailhouse Rock* in December 1956. In Britain, film and television producers were falling over themselves to provide the same kind of entertainment and cash in on the youth bonanza that was clearly coming. *6.5 Special* filled its weekly slot with anything from Terry Dene to Don Lang and His Frantic Five, and the 1958 big-screen version of the television pop programme featured a part-time British rock singer called Jim Dale. To combat the rash of American products like *The Girl Can't Help It* (in which Jayne Mansfield attempts to become a rock singer) or *Rock, Rock, Rock* or *Go, Johnny, Go* or *Untamed Youth* that was spreading like an epidemic, British companies knew it was time to disperse the gloom of Suez and the ire of the angry young men with some homegrown teenpix. With some self-doubt, apparent reluctance and obvious lack of know-how, the rather staid studios finally hitched up their skirts and joined the party in 1957. Originally, *The Tommy Steele Story*[5] had been planned as a wider documentary on British rock 'n' roll, but Parnes and Kennedy had other ideas, and persuaded Anglo-Amalgamated producer Herbert Smith and director Gerard Bryant to add skiffle, calypso and trad jazz...but to focus the lens on Tommy. Bart, Pratt and Steele went along to Decca and began recording the film's score, starting with the flagship 'Handful of Songs', then 'Water Water', 'Freight Train' and the hit single 'Butterfingers', a slow, bassy ballad, which Tommy still rates as one of the best compositions they ever came up with. The movie's screenplay (written by Norman Hudis in ten days) was a pretty formulaic affair about a sarf Lahndan lad buying a guitar from a junk shop, and ending up being discovered by talent scouts in a coffee bar.

As if to keep up a momentum that might be in danger of coming to a sudden halt, the same company engaged Gerald Thomas and Peter Rogers[6] to come up with a sequel. *The Duke Wore Jeans* also has a screenplay by Hudis, though this time 'from a story by Lionel Bart, Michael Pratt'. Hudis claims to have worked closely with the songwriting team 'so that the numbers were an integral part of the entertainment offered and not just arbitrary spots. We were all aware of the challenge of a follow-up to a big success – particularly one based on a real-life success story.' This time, Hudis had the luxury of an entire month to come up with a screenplay in which Tommy plays both a young Duke, called Tony, and his Cockney double, called Tommy, who ends up wooing a European princess for her money. The hat-trick was made the following year with *Tommy the Toreador*. A different creative team nevertheless came up with another dual-identity crisis for trouble-prone Tommy, this time a seaman on shore-leave in Spain who is persuaded by Sid James to take a jailed bullfighter's place in the corrida. Described by one critic as 'a bright, unpolished fiesta', it established Bart beyond any doubt in the pantheon of popular music with a single that Uncle Mac must have despaired of ever removing from the hit parade of Children's Favourites – 'Little White Bull'. Its popular, sentimental melody and fairytale lyrics were part of Tommy's shift from rocker to entertainer. Instead of following Presley's pelvic perversions, his heart was now in the all-round family fare that is still his trademark.

Bart, too, was turning his attentions away from Tin Pan Alley, though not away from teenagers. 'After a couple of years of hits with Tommy and others, we had the charts mastered. We didn't need any market research, we knew what the kids were going to want next week and the week after that. In 1959 I was asked to write four songs for a film called *Serious Charge*,[7] quite a heavy film in which they wanted a delinquent kid who sounded a bit like Presley...and they couldn't find one. Well, I had seen this Harry Webb working with his little band from Cheshunt, and his father was always in tow carrying a little briefcase...and so I put him up to test to be in the film.' Harry was also one of those boys who was unhappy about his given names, but he was eighteen, he was straight from the Presley mould, there was a gap in the market for a rock idol, and his manager, John Foster, told him he needed little else but the pseudonym Cliff Richard. 'If my memory serves, I think I first met Lionel when I played the 2 I's for a week...[8] I knew that Tommy Steele had started in the 2 I's, and so I came to Soho hoping that I'd be discovered as well, but nothing happened. Larry Parnes, Tommy's manager, was out of the country that week, and Lionel was perhaps keeping an eye on things for him. I knew that Lionel had written a lot of Tommy's material, and so I was very much in awe of him. We put him on a pedestal. Then, in the autumn of 1958 things began to happen for me. We got a contract with Columbia, and "Move It" stormed up the charts. So, as a rising young rock 'n' roll star, I was thought to be good casting for the part of Andrew Ray's younger brother in *Serious Charge* and the producer Mickey Delamar hired Lionel to write the songs, which included "Living Doll".[9]

Serious Charge was shot in the last weeks of 1958 at the MGM studios in Borehamwood and on location in Stevenage, and starred Anthony Quayle as a footballing young vicar falsely accused of indecently assaulting one of the juvenile delinquents he is trying to help. Because homosexuality was still a taboo subject, particularly in mainstream cinema, it was decided that its release and popularity would be guaranteed only if it had a contemporary music soundtrack, and a charismatic juvenile or two to draw in a younger audience. Hence, Jess Conrad[9] plays a gang-leader, while Cliff has a small part as Curly, a singer with a group of session musicians.

Among the four songs Lionel came up with for the picture were 'Mad About You', 'No Turning Back' and a fast rhythm number, 'Living Doll', written, he still claims, in under ten minutes one Sunday morning in October 1958, and inspired by a back-page advertisement in the *Sunday Pictorial*, offering, for 99 shillings and sixpence 'The New Improved Darling Doll'. Among its claims for her was that she 'speaks longest and clearest' and 'she KNEELS, walks, sits and sings'. Quite likely,

Bart was also aware of a popular melody from the war years by the Mills Brothers called 'Paper Doll', which contains a lyric about a cut-out paper girl who would not be stolen and would be far more reliable than a real live temptress. For some, Bart's lyric has a sinister side, referring as it does to locking her away in a trunk. For Cliff, it was the unexpected beginning of an endless showbusiness career: 'We recorded it on the soundtrack the way Lionel demo'ed it, which was in a rock 'n' roll fashion, and that's how it appears in the movie. We weren't very happy with the way the song was handled in the film, and when it came to making the record, we felt that we were losing out on the best part of the song...it was actually a very nice song, and so we gave it a country treatment, which took it to number one. It was my first number one, and topped the charts for six weeks in the summer of 1959, and it's still attached to me. It's one of the songs I always have to sing, like "Summer Holiday" or "The Young Ones". It has a simple naiveté which was very much part of the time.' In fact, 'Living Doll' had its first release on a movie-linked EP record, before being put out with the steel guitar sound of his own backing group the Drifters (later to become the Shadows). That single sold a million, helping Cliff to cross the fast-narrowing divide between the rock world and the entertainment universe. It also holds an arcane music-business record as the only song to be released three times by the same artiste. Jack Good, creator of television's pop showcase *Oh Boy!*, still refers to it as his least favourite song ever: 'Its lyrics are twee and its tune trite.'

Lionel too was unstoppable – the golden boy of Tin Pan Alley, winning accolades from his peers each year in the Ivor Novello Awards: three in 1957, four in 1959, and two in 1960 – the year in which he was presented with the Variety Club Silver Heart for Showbusiness Personality of the Year. And he was bored.

CHAPTER THREE

AS LONG AS HE NEEDS ME

But for Ned Sherrin's failure to write a suitable theatrical curtain-raiser for Bernard Miles's new Mermaid Theatre in 1959, Lionel Bart might even now be composing ditties for Eurovision Song Contest hopefuls. Sherrin tells at length[1] how Sir Bernard called him to the construction site of the City of London's first new theatre for 300 years, a permanent stage near Blackfriars Bridge, housed inside a bombed warehouse.[2] These workmen's-hut summits were scheduled on a number of occasions, the Mermaid's founding father having expressed an interest in a musical adaptation of *No Bed for Bacon*, which Sherrin and his veteran partner Caryl Brahms had dramatized from the novel she had written with S. J. Simon. The former music-hall turn turned Mackeson enthusiast was as excited about this Elizabethan comedy of errors as he was about eggs.[3] He was expansive about the play's merits: it was perfect, with its plot about a girl (dressed up as a boy) going to work with Shakespeare, and its setting in the City of London itself. But Bernard, about to leave for America, where he was to appear in a remake of *Wuthering Heights*, demanded rewrite after rewrite, with copious suggestions of his own – including the notion that the entire play be rewritten using only Shakespeare's words and dialogue. Although Sherrin and Brahms may not have been entirely unaware of the fact, Bernard Miles did not think to tell them that he was also having lengthy negotiations with a number of other teams whose brief was to amuse the Queen and Prince Philip on the gala opening at Puddle Dock, a barge's hop from the Tower of London. Without a hint of embarrassment, Miles the theatre-owner eventually settled upon Miles the playwright the task of creating this 'appropriate entertainment' for a monarch notoriously uninterested in the stage.

This was to be an adaptation of an eighteenth-century satire on love and fidelity: Henry Fielding's *Rape Upon Rape,* with music and songs commissioned from Lionel Bart and Laurie Johnson. Miles had looked to Bart, because the latter's *Fings Ain't Wot They Used t'Be* had just opened to some glory at Joan Littlewood's Stratford East – though not without severe birth pangs to accompany its acclaimed arrival.

Frank Norman, although not a Cockney himself, was making a living writing about the East End underworld of gangsters, mobsters and dealers, in an appealing demotic with books like *Bang to Rights*, and in 1958 had written forty-eight pages of dialogue (containing some extremely wayward spelling and countless solecisms), entitled *Fings Ain't Like They Used t'Be*, which he had put away in a drawer and forgotten. It was only after he showed the material to the writer and broadcaster Penelope Gilliat that he was brought into the circle of Joan Littlewood – by then a legendary and tyrannical genius of the theatre, though she had started out as a commercial actress trained at RADA. In 1945 a group of actors had founded Theatre Workshop in Kendal because, according to their manifesto, they were 'dissatisfied with the commercial theatre on artistic, social and political grounds'. Littlewood quickly established herself as artistic director of the new group,[4] which toured Britain and Europe with its 'agitational propaganda' plays and, despite little or no financial backing and no official support, she and her administrator Gerry Raffles finally settled at the derelict Theatre Royal in Chaucer's Stratford-atte-Bowe, in east London. Puzzlingly, Joan herself now claims never to have liked the area: 'Stratford was a rotten place. I was always sorry we went, but it was the only place we could get. I wish to Christ we'd never gone there.' The company, which had a policy of sharing all income equally among members, opened its first production there in February 1953, and built a reputation for honest, hard-hitting work, produced often as a result of Joan's investigative 'improvisational' techniques.

In his book *Why Fings Went West*, Frank Norman recalls his first meeting with Joan and Gerry:

> My impression of Joan Littlewood, when I met her for the first time, was of a solidly built, sympathetic woman in a woolly hat, chain-smoking Gauloises. She greeted me warmly, then we piled into Gerry Raffles's flashy American car and sped off to eat at a Chinese restaurant in Dockland. Over the meal, Joan talked as though *Fings Ain't Wot They Used t'Be* was going into production the following morning, i.e. 'What you've written is marvellous, but I don't think we ought to do it as a straight play, like all that old rubbish those West End managements put on. It should be a musical, or anyway have a few songs in it. I've met this wonderful nutcase called Lionel Bart, I've already talked to him about it and he's agreed to write some songs. What do you think, Frank?'

Joan had met Lionel through Oscar Lewenstein,[5] who had worked with him at Unity Theatre. In fact, Lionel had been a regular visitor to Stratford East, and has often gone on record as having caught the theatre bug from Littlewood's ensemble. By this time Lionel had already written the six core songs of what was to become *Oliver!* and wanted an opinion. Gerry Raffles gave a very positive response, but had engaged him to write a song for each of the Stratford productions, and now had another show that needed Bart's help. 'I was roped in, and had to drop everything and go down to Stratford East and become part of the ensemble. And it was a magic experience. We had two weeks to create this show, and it was totally organic. I'd go home at night, and write three songs that might be needed, and get in next morning and sing them to the company and have to teach them to the company as well as choreograph them.'

According to Joan Littlewood,[6] the company would have to get on without her for a while, since she was busy finding replacements for the transfers of *The Hostage*[7] and *A Taste of Honey*[8], and despite Lionel having

> revived one of his best songs from Unity Theatre days[9]...there was something wrong. On my way to the Angel caff for lunch, I knew what it was. The scenes were written the wrong way round: things would happen, then they'd be discussed...Shaping plays was becoming my speciality. I spent the weekend shuffling the script around and arrived early on the Monday morning with a bundle of pages. We rolled them off and laid out a set of new scripts along the front row of the gallery. From then on, I was hooked on *Fings*. Frank and Lionel were at all the rehearsals, and when more dialogue was needed, they'd be up there ad libbing with the rest of us.

The rewrites continued to mount up, but everyone was galvanized by the songs Lionel was writing on the hoof at the run-throughs and, as Joan admits, the title song itself became the anthem of the Theatre Royal, Stratford East.

For Frank Norman, who had just spent two years at Her Majesty's Pleasure for bouncing cheques, the experience was less than joyful. 'Rehearsals' began even as another section of the company was preparing to open the West End transfer of *A Taste of Honey* in January 1959. In his own book, Norman explains:

> Lionel had already written a few songs, or what he called 'top line and chord symbols' for the show. On the first morning the cast foregathered on stage and the peculiar process began. The famous extemporizing of the actors that had been infused into the text of *The Hostage* and *A Taste of Honey* was now permitted to run riot in *Fings*. With every day that passed, my original conception of the play seemed to drift further and further away, until eventually I was hardly able to identify with the antics on the stage at all. As the weeks went by more songs were added and once in a while I was called upon to write a few more pages of bad language.

Littlewood's technique was perhaps a bastardized version of Stanislavsky mixed up with some Brechtian alienation, but it worked. The company had success upon success, and the martinet at its head had very firm beliefs about the sense of 'ensemble', in which an author was expected to work along with the actors to make drama that was, to pre-empt Peter Brook, 'living theatre'. As she explained in a radio interview that same year: 'I believe very much in a theatre of actor-artists, and I think the trust that comes out of team work on what is often a new script, cleaning up points in production, or contact between actors, is essential to the development of the craft of acting and playwriting.'

Moreover, she was not one to entertain any demarcation lines or class distinctions between performers and providers. According to Lionel, Joan pulled him aside at the interval on the first night, saying she needed a song for the second half to show the menace of the antagonist called Meat Face, who remained unseen, but whose very name instilled terror whenever it was heard. Lionel was to go on stage as a busker, and sing an impromptu song about this character at three different cues in the second act. And legend seems to support the claim that Lionel, having found an old First World War greatcoat and oversize boots under the stage, pulled on a battered hat, blacked out a tooth, sketched out a tune and went on singing 'Meat Face...who ran away with the blind man's hat, Meat Face, Meat Face...who does a murder just like that...Meat Face...' And for two weeks, Lionel stopped his own show, after which George Sewell, travel courier turned bit-part actor, took over.

Fings opened with a roar on Tuesday 17 February 1959, and had instant appeal to its raffish local audience, who appreciated not only its colour, but its language that came not from a Shavian drawing-room, but direct from the streets on which they did their 'business'. Norman had set his action in a seedy little gambling-den, run by ex-members of a razor gang and their attendant pimps, prossies and protectors. Perhaps Ms Littlewood had accurately sensed a restive mood among jaded theatregoers and critics alike, who 'seemed to be as bored with drawing-room theatre as we were. They enjoyed identifying themselves with these ponces, lags and layabouts. Frank's language, learned on the streets, in the nick or in Soho spielers, was a change from the drama school cockney, suitable for faithful batmen and moronic maids.' However, for some audiences and for some critics, the larger-than-life authenticity was just too rough to handle. Even a meeting of the Theatre Royal Supporters' Club heard complaints that it was all too outspoken and sordid; a more real concern was expressed about the morality of using razor gangs and prostitutes as subjects for satirical songs: such stigmatization was surely little better than sending up the poor, the mentally ill or the physically deformed. One critic penned a lament for the passing of 'decent' entertainment: 'Love with no tattered strings, kindness, hope, faith and common decency are no longer the thing. Banished are the musicals such as came from the Lehárs and the Novellos who gave us such wonderful shows.'

From the pages of the *Daily Express* came an unlikely champion of the attractions of the kitchen sink:[10] Bernard Levin simply acknowledged *Fings* as 'a play of brilliant, bawdy irreverence'. Caryl Brahms, though, writing decidedly unstylishly in *Plays and Players*, refused to be impressed:

> The play is lively if purposeless. The scene, which is a Soho gaming club, conscientiously teems with the entrances and exits of a cast of character actors devotedly doing their nut. The staging is Littlewood utility. The play is punctuated with songs (if punctuation means stopped by) thrown into what ought to be the action like currants into dough and seemingly without much more premeditation... The author has a quick enough ear for dialogue but he must dig his foundations a bit deeper and so enable himself to build his edifice to the point. There were of course some good things in the picture of Soho cellarage...I wish I could have liked it better. I wish I could have liked it period.

Brahms also pointed out that the theatre had managed to draw a fair proportion of its patrons from 'young Chelsea' who, doubtless in search of some contact with Soho without the dangers of actually being there, had travelled east out of a certain *nostalgie de la boue*. They, and others, continued to fill the house for six or seven weeks, enabling Gerry Raffles to raise wages to £20 a week, and encouraging Joan to revive the production at the Theatre Royal for a fortnight on 7 April and for a further seven-week run on 22 December. To name the names which Joan Littlewood 'discovered' at Stratford is now part of theatre folklore, but from that 1959 company came the likes of Richard Harris, James Booth, Yootha Joyce and Miriam Karlin, who took over from Avis Bunnage in the third revival of *Fings*, earning £15 a week for singing 'The Ceilin's Coming Dahn'. 'I had longed to work for Joan Littlewood, and one day she rang me to ask if I would be interested, but kept assuming I wouldn't want to do it, because I was "West End". But I was over the moon, I was so excited, and it was an amazing experience in that for the first time one could legitimately improvise, it was just the most wondrous process. I always used to say, don't go to the loo while rehearsing with Joan...you'll come back and find you've lost your part.'[11]

But Joan was also responsible for finding new players, sometimes from unlikely sources, such as Danny La Rue's nightclub Winston's. Already Victor Spinetti was straddled across the two Ends – West and East – and he was shortly joined by two of the showgirls, Barbara Windsor and Toni Palmer, who spent the first half of the evening in grit and the second half in glitter, and who quickly learned that the 'improvisation lark' might mean prancing around the stage as a horse. During those rehearsals for *Fings* Joan was her usual unyielding self, even though the show had enjoyed two successful productions. 'She would come in and watch something we'd spent three days on and say "Scrap it, it's awful, it doesn't work." And she'd start again, take numbers out, put them in, get writers to rewrite. She couldn't work with people who were precious about their work and didn't allow input from the actors and from herself. She used to give us colour-coded notes, pinned up around a room, exquisitely hand-printed, sometimes with alternate letters in different colours. One day Barbara got fed up and wrote on hers, DON'T FUCKING AGGRAVATE ME, JOAN, I'VE GOT ENOUGH PROBLEMS. Joan thought that was hysterically funny.'

Within a week of its first night, eight or nine West End managements were interested in transferring the show, and it finally moved to the Garrick on 11 February 1960, which remained its home until late February 1962. And Lionel almost felt it was his right. 'It was my first West End show, but right from the beginning, it was set to go. The audience were behind it. There was huge laughter in the theatre, and it already had a kind of following before we even opened in town. It became a kind of cult for a while.' And, legitimately, it is generally acknowledged to be Lionel's contribution, as composer and lyricist, that accounted for *Fings* winning the 1960 Evening Standard Award for Best Musical – though this did little to impress the official theatre censor, the Lord Chamberlain. Since the opening at Stratford, the street offences act (which dealt with prostitution) had become law, and the play required some updating. Out, also, had gone quite a number of the expletives that had survived unnoticed in the territory of their everyday use, thus appeasing the West End audiences and Westminster by reducing considerably the number of sod-offs, bugger-offs and piss-offs. Yet, curiously, twelve months had elapsed without incident, when the following letter was received by the Garrick management.

The Lord Chamberlain's Office,
St James's Palace, S.W.1.   7th February 1961

Dear Sir,

The Lord Chamberlain has received numerous complaints against the play *Fings Ain't Wot They Used t'Be* in consequence of which he arranged for an inspection of the Garrick Theatre to be made on 1st of February last.

It is reported to his Lordship that numerous unauthorized amendments to the allowed manuscript have been made, and I am to require you to revert to it at once, submitting for approval any alteration which you wish to make before continuing them in use.

In particular, I am to draw your attention to the undernoted, none of which would have been allowed had they been submitted, and which I am to ask you to confirm by return of post have been removed from the play.

ACT I

Indecent business of Rosie putting her hand up Red Hot's bottom.

The dialogue between Rosie and Bettie. 'You've got a cast iron stomach.' 'You've got to have in our business.'

The interior decorator is not to be played as a homosexual and his remark '...Excuse me dear, red plush, that's very camp, that is,' is to be omitted, as is the remark, 'I've strained meself.'

The builder's labourer is not to carry the plank of wood in the erotic place and at the erotic angle that he does, and the Lord Chamberlain wishes to be informed of the manner in which the plank is in future to be carried.

ACT II

The reference to the Duchess of Argyll is to be omitted. Tosher, when examining Red Hot's bag, is not to put his hand on Rosie's bottom with finger aligned as he does at the moment.

The remark, 'Don't drink that stuff, it will rot your drawers,' is to be omitted.

Tosher is not to push Rosie backwards against the table when dancing in such a manner that her legs appear through his open legs in a manner indicative of copulation.

Yours faithfully,

The letter, now little more than an indication of the ridicule and contempt the Lord Chamberlain's office inspired, is signed by Assistant Comptroller, Lieutenant-Colonel E. Penn on behalf of Lord Scarborough. 'And the funny thing is,' Miriam Karlin told the *Daily Mail*, 'the Lord Chamberlain has seen the play twice and thoroughly enjoyed it, to judge by his laughter. Most of the material they want out has been used from the beginning. It isn't a question of a lot of things having crept into the script.'

Bart, who had been handed the letter by Donald Albery at a dinner party on stage to celebrate the first anniversary, was equally baffled when woken at 1.15 p.m. on the Sunday after the beano. 'It's the most incredible state of affairs I've ever known.' Because there was no appeal against the censor's decisions, Bart would, reluctantly, have to change the proclivities of the interior decorator, but claimed he would make it clear that the poor chap 'used to work for the Lord Chamberlain's office and only took up decorating after he got the sack, see?'

Experiment was in the air at Puddle Dock, situated geographically to the west of Stratford, but spiritually as far away from Shaftesbury Avenue as Joan's demotic bunker. In its June 1959 issue, *Plays and Players* paid encomiastic tribute to their anointed leader of the 'new theatre' with the words:

> Bernard Miles has done something more than just build a new theatre in London: he has brought new hope to the whole art of drama in this country. Playhouses may be going dark in the West End and throughout the country, but a new light has appeared in the heart of the City itself – hitherto a dark, dreary waste every evening.

Miles was also a genius for encouraging patrons to wine and dine, to stay on after a show and discuss the performances; for his battlecry of two meals and two seats for £1; for his plans to have lunchtime concerts, film shows and jazz festivals... even for his choice of plays. While Shaftesbury Avenue's patrons had recently lapped up Tommy Steele as Buttons in *Cinderella*[12] and were now bringing good business to *West Side Story*,[13] and Paul Scofield's award-winning performance in *Expresso Bongo*,[14] Bernard proposed alternative delights like the *Wakefield Mysteries* and Marc Connelly's *The Green Pastures*, since both were under the censor's ban at the time. Even his unorthodox means of attracting publicity – a Tiller Girls' race, barbecues on the building site, a triumphal opening ceremony – raised a smile rather than a frown. He never relinquished the belief that 'actors should bang the drums and march through the streets'.

As his first resident producer, Bernard Miles had appointed a twenty-nine-year-old former actor, Peter Coe. In its first interview with him, a few weeks ahead of the opening, *Plays and Players* published a discursive interview with the new broom, describing him thus: 'A young director with fixed and controversial ideas on the growth of the theatre, Coe brings to this project in the City something more than the necessary number of years in provincial repertory. Tall, bearded and fine-eyed, he has all the outward appearance of a theatre fanatic but his infectious enthusiasm is firmly grounded on wide experience.'

Coe had first trained in stagecraft at LAMDA,[15] where he later taught, before running provincial repertory theatres at Ipswich, Farnham, Carlisle and Lincoln. What Bernard Miles wanted from him were 'ideas and ideals' which would make the Mermaid not only a new theatre, but the breeding ground for a new concept of drama in the country. In its construction, the Mermaid is like a dish, with a 48-foot platform stage blending the acting area with the audience. This, Coe was in favour of, as his model was 'always to work on an open stage, moving from situation to situation without the restrictions of a proscenium set'. The belief, at that time anyway, was that a wide, uninterrupted acting area would provide a freer atmosphere, as well as bringing the audience 'into the spirit of the play'. It was a universal dramaturgical panacea, which architects, producers, directors and actors faithfully imagined would induce active concern among playgoers, rather than the passive enjoyment to which, presumably, they were no longer entitled. This trend owed something to Eastern theatre practice, where actors and audiences would casually engage in dialogue and debate across the footlights, breaking down even the mental barrier between acting and reacting, and moreover, it was anticipated that this influence would also promote the singer–actor, 'a phenomenon surprisingly difficult to find in the English theatre' at that time.

Absolutely made for Coe was the stage designer Sean Kenny: their ideals and dramatic beliefs could not have chimed more harmoniously. In many ways, Kenny was a maverick, who had sailed a converted shrimper over to America in order to study architecture with the twentieth-century icon Frank Lloyd Wright. After trying his hand at gold-panning, sub-aqua filming and life on an Indian reservation, he practised architecture in Canada and his native Ireland. The Lyric Theatre in London's Hammersmith housed his first theatre work, which led to his involvement with Joan Littlewood, for whom he designed the sets for Brendan Behan's *The Hostage*. From here, he was invited to create the setting for *Lock Up Your Daughters*, and that show's instant success led to his appointment as first resident art director at the Mermaid, where the opening souvenir book contains his utopian message for drama: 'Let us rebel, fight, break down, invent and reconstruct a new theatre.

Let us free the theatre from the cumbersome shackles of outmoded traditions.'

No stage designer identified himself with the new movement in English theatre more closely than Sean Kenny, thanks particularly to his willingness to dispense with elaborate scenery in favour of a minimum of simple designs, imaginatively lit. 'Lighting is a very important part of the visual picture. It is not something that you add on afterwards. For example, four poles and a platform may look simple by themselves on a stage, but you can light them to look like a bed, or a boxing ring or a mountain. Lighting is the third dimension of design – and the actor is the fourth. That is why, when I design, I must put figures on the sets. A set must be designed as a whole, otherwise all you get are bits and pieces that may certainly be interesting, but will still be a conglomeration of different people's ideas.'

The Mermaid's opening season plans bore voluble testament to this artistic pairing and to their eclectic – some might say slightly dotty – policies, with its mix of *Journey's End, Great Expectations, Treasure Island,*[16] *Antigone,* Brecht's *Galileo,* Camus' *Les Justes.* And, under the new concrete roof, rehearsals were underway for *Lock Up Your Daughters.* A more 'period' piece could not be imagined: sexual liberation had not quite dawned, and the pre-feminist sentiments of even the title song would today raise more than an eyebrow and less than a titter.

Dispassionately (and politically asexually) considered, Bart's lyrics have a tongue-twisting charm and ingenuity, but add the opening refrain to numbers like 'A Proper Man', 'Red Wine and a Wench', 'Lovely Lover' and 'When Does the Ravishing Begin?' (which Hy Hazell as Mrs Squeezum, the corrupt magistrate's shameless wife, began with a confession of lost virtue) and an almost seedy spectacle starts to emerge from the harmless musical comedy – at least on paper, since there are no ravishings visible on stage. Our heroine Hilaret (played voluptuously by Stephanie Voss) is rarely far from danger, and falls in – perhaps a shade too willingly on occasion – with a catalogue of pimps, ruffians and corrupt judges, but the show remains as wholesome as a Benny Hill sketch.

That regal evening of Thursday 28 May 1959 was awash with goodwill and warm sentiment, in some contrast to the morning newspapers, which were filled with the bile of Liberace's ongoing libel suit against the *Daily Mirror* and the people of York demanding the immediate removal of a priapic Epstein statue from the Minster. The Mermaid's opening night began with a river ceremony, in which the tiny daughter of Jack Hawkins, wrapped in a shawl, was rowed ashore by sea cadets, and toasted on to the bank by the Lord Mayor of London. Beneath the stage a casket was buried, containing the names of the theatre's sub-scribers. In one report, a somewhat patronizing account of the local theatregoers emerged: 'The audience, largely drawn from the east of Temple Bar, obviously approved a spacious foyer with its several bars.' And the critics, clearly not a breed to be wooed by foyer bars, found themselves moved to praise this 'roaring musical'. Bill Lester, reviewing the event in *Plays and Players*, put it into context: 'Of course it's im-proper. But it's alive, which is more than you can say for any other British musical at present.' Noting that 'zest' was the keynote of the act-ing, Bill wonders why he detected the rhythm of the Cha-cha-cha a couple of centuries too soon, but rounds off with a tribute to 'particu-larly bright, explicit lyrics'. The *Times* notice also mentions the 'spirited lyrics of Mr Lionel Bart and the charmingly gay music of Mr Laurie Johnson'.

Within hours of the curtain ringing down, Bernard Miles decided there was only one course of action: extend the run to 8 August. It was not enough to satisfy an audience with a thirst for the slightly titivating, and the show transferred to Her Majesty's for a run of sixteen months.

Lionel now had two shows running concurrently in the West End. Barely twelve months earlier, he had been composing throwaway songs for one-hit wonders to clamber on to the lower rungs of the charts. Nobody was surprised, least of all the newly cocksure Lionel, when Hollywood thought it smelled success and started to put in bids, using the old formula of nothing succeeds like excess. The price they quoted for *Daughters* was £100,000 plus. Lionel, now the assured negotiator, decided to hold out, waiting for them to go up another couple of thou.

With a horrible, unwitting prescience, Shirley Flack in the popular press tells her readers that Lionel can, after all, afford to wait. 'If he never did another day's work, he would be able to live in luxury for the rest of his days.'

CHAPTER FOUR

WHO WILL BUY?

At the beginning of the new year and the new decade, Bart was busy. Busy preparing to break a record by having three musical shows running in the West End at the same time: the transfer to Broadway and the London revival of *Lock Up Your Daughters*, the transfer from Stratford of *Fings*, and the spring opening of *Oliver!* It was songwriting that was bankrolling him: without a touch of embarrassment, Bart candidly told one newspaper how much he enjoyed money: 'I like nothing better than lying back in my bath and hearing myself earn £3 in four minutes on *Housewives' Choice*; four minutes being the time it took for the average pop record to play, £3 being his share of the royalties.

Following the success of the Tommy Steele movies, Bart had originally conceived and written a few *Oliver!* songs for the chirpy heartthrob with an eye to making another film. Tommy, though, was both too old to play the ten-year-old Artful Dodger and too young to play Fagin and, in any case, along came *Fings* to steal a lead over the unfinished ideas. Neither was Dickens's underworld melodrama quite the racy vehicle Lionel intended to bring to the stage, so he chose to focus on the more eventful first section of the novel – the boy's early years, up to the point where Oliver leaves the workhouse to find unimaginable riches and happiness. Three-quarters of the book were, in the process, abandoned as unsuitable, and the resulting 'book' of the musical is described by Bart himself as being 'freely adapted' from the clotted Victorian inspiration.

The image of Oliver had always been a childhood icon for Lionel. He remembered a little sweet shop opposite his parents' house in the East End where they sold a chocolate bar with a toffee inside for a penny. It was called 'Oliver',[1] and the wrapper around it had a picture of a lad asking for more. When it came to the idea for a musical, the twenty-nine-year-old Bart was looking for a big, lusty story, and decided that Dickens's *Oliver Twist* had certain key ingredients. The Dickens hero, though, was a bit frail, and needed to become a lad with more spirit. Not that there wasn't a danger in tampering with the popular, cherished classics – as he was to find out to his almighty cost with a show five years later...

Bart could hardly claim to be the first to see the theatrical potential of Dickens's novel. Shortly after the book's publication in 1838 there had been a dramatization, and the author himself toured both Britain and America giving lectures, and reading aloud passages from the novel. Such was Dickens's passion and his audience's emotional susceptibility that, on hearing the section about Nancy's murder, ladies had a tendency to faint.

Oliver Twist, however, as Bart knew, was more than a book – it was a tradition. It had also been made familiar by several films – most famously with Jackie Coogan in 1922, a forgotten 1933 version and David Lean's matchless 1948 picture starring Alec Guinness, Robert Newton and Bart's friend Anthony Newley as Dodger. Some cavillers in 1959 were already asking if this was going to be 'Rockin' Round the Gruel Bowl'. The idea was taken round to various managements, nearly all the producers in London, and it was turned down. Twelve managements rejected the chance to buy the rights, while the publishing deal for the music eventually went to Max Bygraves' company Lakeview Music for just £1,000.[2] These supposedly imaginative producers and backers all told Bart that a story about children exploited in a workhouse and Nancy beaten to death was 'too morbid'. One of them was convinced the show wouldn't work because it lacked a gimmick; he suggested 'an all-coloured cast'.

Finally, on the strength only of Bart's own tape recording (featuring the composer, his secretary Joan Maitland and a friend performing all the parts), Donald Albery took an option on the unfinished show, with Peter Coe to direct and Sean Kenny to design, and bought and staged *Oliver!* for just £15,000. Partly it was an act of faith; partly it was Albery's belief in the team that had successfully produced a lucrative transfer for him from the Mermaid. Lionel was delighted to be reunited with the director and designer who had collaborated on *Lock Up Your Daughters*. Casting was to be entirely under his control; or at least that was how he saw it.

Albery did not share the same vision, and as plans progressed a chasm widened between them. Composer and producer had originally agreed that a star name was required to guarantee a box-office advance, and possibles for the role of Fagin began to be discussed. Among those who politely refused the invitation were Rex Harrison, Sid James and Peter Sellers. When the list was exhausted, they decided to hold open auditions. Nothing emerged to satisfy the increasingly conflicting demands of the two progenitors, until Coe came up with a suggestion. Why not let an inexperienced young actor have a crack at the part? His name? Ronald Moodnick, by birth, but known to Equity and his audiences as Ron Moody. Albery and Bart were, at best, sceptical. But when Albery ultimately chose to put his weight behind Moody, Lionel could do little to stop the casting going ahead. 'I'd only ever seen Ron Moody do impersonations and things like that at the Talk of the Town, and I did think he was a very versatile revue performer. When we told him he had to play this Jewish mother-hen – a cross between a leprechaun and a pied-piper – he handled it very well. He went straight into gear with it, and there *was* nobody else after his audition.'

Nancy, too, was proving tough to cast. The known galaxies failed to provide a star, and another audition was held, which this time threw up Lilian Klot, a girl Lionel had known since childhood in the East End, though she had now decided to be known as Georgia Brown (one newspaper, unfamiliar with her new name, referred to her throughout as Georgina[3]). Another unknown called Michael Caine was auditioned (for the part of Sikes) and 'cried for days' when he found he'd been unsuccessful, though even now he claims he might still be in endless West End runs if he had been selected. For the 'lesser' parts of Oliver and the Dodger, very public open auditions were held, frequently for the exclusive benefit of press photographers. There had been talk of recruiting Dickie Pride from the Larry Parnes rock-boy stable; on 18 February 1960 an advertisement appeared in the *Stage*, outlining the requirements for a suitable juvenile; a month later, the *Daily Sketch* begged its readers to come up with a boy who 'must *look* about thirteen'; in the pages of *Radio Review*, Marion Ryan was advising Bart to pick Wee Willie Harris as Dodger. Finally, from around a hundred hopefuls, freckle-faced fourteen-year-old Keith Hamshere from Ilford turned up. Although he had once performed a song-and-dance routine alongside Bud Flanagan in *The Crazy Gang Show*, Keith could hardly have foreseen the adulation to come...and go just as quickly. His oppo as Dodger was another fourteen-year old, Martin Horsey, whose father could not have been more central casting: he ran a coffee stall in Bermondsey.

With the major parts now allocated, it was still some time before the musical went into rehearsal at the Donmar rooms, a former banana warehouse in London's Covent Garden market, and which was then a warehouse for Albery's theatres: the Wyndham's, the Piccadilly, the Criterion and the New (now the Albery). The company was there for three weeks, sharing the run-down space with scaffolding and lumber.

Bart started the show with just the six songs he had written, and then recorded them with Joan Maitland and others: 'Food, Glorious Food', 'I'd Do Anything', 'Reviewing the Situation', 'Consider Yourself', 'Who Will Buy?' and 'As Long As He Needs Me'. He wrote most of the other songs at the end of the rehearsal period, and a few more in the ten days they had at Wimbledon Theatre[4] – including 'That's Your Funeral' for Barry Humphries, who was cast as the undertaker.[5] The run-up to Wimbledon was fraught and frantic. They realized that the theatre was close enough

41

to allow word-of-mouth – good or bad – to seep back to Shaftesbury Avenue. Nevertheless, the first out-of-town night appears to have run without a hitch, and was followed by supper for Lionel, Ron Moody, the actress Vivienne Martin and one or two others in their colleague Thelma Ruby's splendid house overlooking Wimbledon Park Golf Club. Moody, though, doesn't have entirely happy recollections about the previews. 'I remember when we did the show first at Wimbledon it wasn't *terribly* successful...nobody seemed very impressed. After two weeks, there was a short break, we went to the New, and Peter Coe allowed me to do whatever I wanted. And the only note he gave me was "Now make it real."'

During the run at Wimbledon Coe was also giving notes to the composer, asking Bart to write reprises and music to accompany some of the action sequences, particularly those involving the transformations of the stage's multi-level revolving core – in a way like processing music to film action. It was something new in the theatre, one of the many innovations in the production. Sean Kenny was hailed by Bart as 'a genius, a hundred years ahead of fashion, certainly of his time'. The music for the scene changes meant that one of the best places to see the show was from the top of the gallery: a vision of a great moving ballet of pieces of machinery and stage construction, which had required 4,000 feet of timber and steel. Kenny described the preparative work for the show which first brought him to the attention of the general theatregoing public. 'I steeped myself in Dickens and in the City of London. I walked round there and did hundreds of sketches and then made a rough model. Later Peter Coe and I worked out a final model incorporating all his production ideas. As we worked together on this musical, he found he wanted different designs, and they changed with his ideas – and his ideas with mine until it finally came out as one piece. I think that the way we worked on *Oliver!* is probably the right one. One should not design too much for effect, too much for visual appearance. The design must grow out of the musical itself. And actors should not stop acting while something changes on the set, and then start acting again. The thing should run through, follow through as a camera does in a film. The idea is to try to stop the idea that everybody should wait while the scene changes.

The stage should be free from that – and if we have to get rid of scenery and just use lighting, then we will have to do just that. We must put a stop to all this business of big heavy trucks coming in and darkness for half an hour while they change the flats behind the curtain. That sort of thing is an example of the tail wagging the dog. We must get rid of canvas, of pseudo-marble painted on wallpaper and all that kind of thing.'

And yet it was because of one of those pieces of Kenny's innovative machinery that the London first night almost opened in disaster. The run-ups had been gruelling for the entire team, both on-stage and off. Rewrites had been going on up to the last morning of previews, songs were being added and removed, choruses lengthened and shortened, the curtain-calls cancelled and restored. Bearing in mind that so many changes had been made, the company had had only the ten days of pre-views in Wimbledon, which meant that the opening in London was more or less 'cold' – there was no chance to run the show or to ease it into an unfamiliar theatre with new crews and a new stage. The opening was to be on Thursday 30 June 1960, in the middle of a heatwave. Only a few nights previously the entire ending of the show had been altered. After the murder at London Bridge and the chase of Bill Sikes and his dog, Bart had written a scene back at the workhouse where the Artful Dodger is saved and Oliver brings him back with his benefactor with a handful of gifts for the ragamuffins – a short scene with snatches of reprised songs in it. However, it proved mechanically impossible to strike London Bridge, so it was decided to bring the lights up, kill all the dialogue and sing those reprises...and, according to Mr Bart, that is how the sung curtain-call came about. It is also, arguably, thanks to Bart that the hit single of a show is now released well in advance of the opening night. In this case, Max Bygraves (still warm from his success with the release of the title song from *Fings*) had released Dodger's stirring friend-ship anthem 'Consider Yourself', and a fortnight before the show's offi-cial West End opening night Shirley Bassey was in the *New Musical Express* charts with the song that was to become her theme tune, 'As Long As He Needs Me'. Reputedly, she has harboured a lifelong dislike of the work.

By the morning of the press show at the New, Bart was as exhausted as any of them, but he still managed to find time at around 11 a.m. for an interview with Herbert Kretzmer,[6] now also better known as a lyricist than a journalist. In the *Sunday Dispatch* feature, which appeared three days after opening night, Bart is photographed in a four-button blazer, white cuff-linked shirt and self-satisfied grin, looking backwards over the driving seat of 'his £4,250 Mercedes convertible' with personalized number plate LB 4. The price excluded the cost of a 'built-in telephone'. He had just sold his MGA saloon, was keeping the Volkswagen Karmann-Ghia (price £1,250, and always known as a 'lady's car') for 'nipping around town', and as a stand-by maintained a Riley Pathfinder. Yet, in Kretzmer's words: 'The most successful British songwriter since Ivor Novello and Noël Coward is a small, dark, ex-slum dweller with a chip on his shoulder, three cars in the garage and an income of something like £50,000 a year. His name is Lionel Bart. It is an easy name to remember, and that's the way Bart likes it. He writes songs that are easy to remember, too.'

In spite of the build-up, and in spite of what seemed already like permanent financial security, Lionel was on edge about the prospect of *Oliver!*'s première later that day. 'I tell you straight, mate, if anything goes wrong on the stage tonight, I'm going to walk out of the theatre and wander round Trafalgar Square until it's all over.' Bart toyed with his tea cup, and nervously stubbed out a hardly smoked cigarette. 'I am always worrying about what comes next. It's a dodgy lark, I tell you. Some people get dizzy with success. Not me. I get apprehensive. That's it. Apprehensive. The phone never stops ringing. I am inundated with offers. People want me to write songs for shows, songs for films. But listen, mate, I've got to know what to take on, what to turn down. It's a headache. I have just rejected a Hollywood offer to write all the songs for Elvis Presley's next picture. I need something big and exciting to be working on. I can't repeat myself, see? That's fatal. Everything I do must be bigger and better than anything I have done before. That's my kick, mate.'

And at that point the white ivory telephone at Bart's elbow tinkles. Kretzmer allows his listeners a moment's harmless eavesdropping. '*Who*

wants seats for the show? Lord *Whom*? OK, tell him he can have two.'
Which all went to show how hard it was to become to see the hit musical of the era... Lionel lights another cigarette, and continues the homily.
'Basically, I am successful because I approach songwriting as a performer. I never write into a void. I always know just who I am writing a
song for. I work to his individual style and audience. I put myself in his
shoes. When I write a Tommy Steele song, like "Handful of Songs", I
write it for Tommy and nobody else, get it? It works out that way, mate,
it really does. I still can't read a note of music. Can't play a note either.
When I compose a song I just hum it into a tape recorder. Then somebody else puts down the dots on paper. What's the difference, mate? It's
working out, isn't it?' It most definitely was – though Lionel did not
seem a particularly contented person that day. 'I was happier when I was
playing washboard for Tommy Steele in the early days and loafin' around
Soho with fifteen bob in my pocket...'

It was no day for regret. Immediately after lunch, Lionel went to the
New Theatre to reassure himself that the walk round Trafalgar Square
wouldn't be necessary. Late in the afternoon he rushed home to Reece
Mews to change into black tie, and was back at the theatre by six, flap-
ping and checking everything, yet hugging and reassuring his team. As
the overture began, he took his seat – on the aisle so that he could nip
out to the bar or backstage during the lighting black-outs which he
knew by heart. The audience didn't notice, and the cast couldn't see
him slipping in and out.

A little over three hours later Bart gorged himself on the delirium in
the wings, being kissed, back-slapped and hand-pumped until he took
his curtain-call to a public that had witnessed nothing like it since
Oklahoma! came to town. 'When I stepped on the stage I felt a gigantic
wave of love coming over the footlights. It was physically staggering.' As
one who witnessed the moment described it: 'Bart accepted the idolatry
with a series of thin, nervous grins. Sweat filmed his forehead. He glis-
tened like a garden gnome after a shower...' Ron Moody shares the same
feeling about the buzz of that evening: 'There was an enormous zing
from that first-night audience. The curtain-calls went on and on, there
was a kind of electrical magnetism around the theatre. I've never known

it since. It's what they call success...but it's more than that...it's excitement...it sizzled.'

The 'society pages' of the newspapers next day showed Lionel arriving at the theatre with Letitzia Adam, Jackie Lane and Lionel Blair. In the 22s and 6d stalls seats were Rex Harrison, only a few hours after his return from America, Sandra Caron (Alma Cogan's sister), Max Bygraves, film director Lewis Gilbert, singers Glen Mason and Jess Conrad, and Judy Carne. A fortnight later, Rex was back again, this time with Tammy Grimes on his arm and a two-fingered salute to the photographers on the other. Princess Margaret with Antony Armstrong-Jones and four friends turned up at the beginning of August, followed later in the year by her own sister, the Queen, who made two visits within two weeks, and (needless to say, not on the same occasion) by the Duke and Duchess of Windsor. There was no stopping it. Everyone wanted More!

True, some critics *had* been as ecstatic as that first-night audience, whose warmth was captured the next day by the *Daily Sketch*, which began: 'A warming, wonderful thing to hear last night. Resounding, uproarious cheers for a British musical – roars of pleasure from stalls and gallery in unison.' And the *Daily Herald* had no doubts, to judge from its headline, 'OLIVER TWIST? GIVE ME MORE!' But there was no unanimity of consent or congratulation from that first morning's papers, read to Bart, some of them selectively, over the telephone by friends and members of the company. Although Bernard Levin and the *Express* were with him, the *Guardian* and its slightly rearguard critic Philip Hope-Wallace were having none of it: '...a sad disappointment, a very starveling musical from the workhouse... There is no denying a certain gutter-sparrow charm about it.' *Time and Tide*'s Richard Findlater did not even allow it to charm: 'Among the disappointments of *Oliver!* is the failure of Lionel Bart's score to reach the peaks even of pastiche melodrama.' As for the regional press, while the *Birmingham Post* was predicting 'it will be very difficult to follow *Oliver!*' the *Oxford Mail* was more cautiously announcing 'a good show but not a superlative one'. Intriguingly, beneath the headline 'THIS FAGIN IS UNIQUE', the *Jewish Chronicle* made the point that 'it lacks humour and dancing' (doubtless mirroring the paper itself). Dismissing Ron Moody as a 'benzedrine Shylock', the *Spectator's* critic Alan Brien decides that the trouble with *Oliver!* is that it has no guts, and is little more than a 'tasty strip-cartoon fillet...served with a thin, sugared gruel of words and music oddly enough ladled from almost the same pot as *Follow That Girl*.[7] And he offers some advice to the composer. 'What Lionel Bart needs now is a bloody, bawdy, outrageous, unspeakable injustice to start some adrenaline pumping into his words and music – he should set his next production in a blackboard jungle or a colonial prison camp.' Taking up the theme in his *Observer* column a week later, Ken Tynan predicts the future Dickens musicals *Bleak!, David!, Great!* and *Jack's the Boy!*, 'loosely derived from the Whitechapel murders of half a century ago'. In fact, it was to be only a matter of weeks before Russ Conway and Bernard Delfont were announcing, in Tynan's own paper, their plans to stage *A Christmas Carol*.

Within those first twenty-four hours, however, it had dawned on almost everybody, as it had on Alan Brien, that '*Oliver!* should keep Lionel Bart in petrol and caviare'. Overnight, ticket agency deals worth £22,000 were confirmed: having taken only £130 in advance bookings up to opening night, the box office took £600 in the first morning alone. Five transatlantic offers arrived for a Broadway transfer, plus one cable. David Merrick was among the bidders. Kermit Bloomgarden flew in to London to inspect the goods on offer. Meanwhile, half a dozen London impresarios kicked themselves hard in the pants for missing the show what was offered to *them* two years earlier.

For twenty years, from 1973 until 1994, Lionel Bart did not receive a penny piece from it other than a author's royalty.

As ever, the movie business was eager to capitalize on the success of a stage show with a tried and proven audience-drawing formula. Within six months of his spectacular hit opening at the New Theatre on St Martin's Lane, Lionel Bart was being offered $2 million (£714,000 at the time) by Hollywood for the film rights. It was the largest sum ever put up for an option. But Bart was uncertain about accepting. 'It just happens to be the biggest of many offers I have had. Nearly every

English film company has been after the rights, but I don't think they could do it on their own.' He was confident he could hold out for a better deal, one in which he would keep control over casting and make sure it was shot in England. According to Lionel's manager, Jock Jacobson, negotiations had been going on for more than a month, but nothing definite had been decided. Bart had been stalling over full artistic authority, and insisting on Danny Kaye to play Fagin, with Judy Garland as Nancy.

Meanwhile, Max Bygraves, president of the company which had bought the musical rights to the score for £1,000, was considering his own good fortune. 'We bought these songs quite innocently, thinking they would not be a bad deal. Of course, that was before Lionel hit the big-time. I suppose we took a chance on the music – but we knew he had the touch of success.' And Max went on to reveal the price of that success: he had been offered $25,000 (around £9,000) by Twentieth Century–Fox for the film rights of the music score alone. And yet Max too was less than eager to settle: 'It is too big to sell yet. We are holding the aces, and everybody is after it. There has never been a musical like this.'

And how Lionel knew it!

A mere sixteen weeks after the opening of the show that has ever after been synonymous with him, the East End barrow-boy is at his Kensington mews apartment. Its layout is compact, chic and comfortable. The flower arrangement in the corner is a classic, the work of expert hands. A cigarette box and table lamp are by another classicist, Fornasetti. To one side of the room, a cocktail cabinet stocked with the finest champagnes and cognacs. And, looking still a little out of synch with the elegance of his store-bought surroundings, Lionel in an embroidered dress-shirt (it was the middle of the afternoon), pencil tight trousers and sporting a brand new profile – a snip at £150! Lionel had spent some of his *Oliver!* profits on a nose job. And in 1960 few men would have admitted to having a nip and tuck of the proboscis. In fact, not until Tom Jones smoothed the edges was it considered anything but effete vanity for a man to want to change his appearance with plastic surgery. Even Lionel's mother made mockery of her son's reduced organ: 'It is a big family joke. I keep asking him, Lionel, where is the long nose?'

Mother seemed convinced that success hadn't changed her boy – except for his name and his nose. And like every good Jewish matriarch, she was beginning to think she might be even happier if the boy showed some sign of getting married. 'He says it wouldn't be fair on a girl, because he has to travel and be out late at night. Lionel would never be unfair to a girl. He is as generous with his love as with his money.'

Certainly he was out to spend some of it on a new home in Kensington, St John's Wood, Knightsbridge or Mayfair, and began the search through the estate agent Blake & Co. of Mount Street, Mayfair, with £40,000 in his pocket. But was it enough? 'You'd have thought it wouldn't be all that difficult to get something nice for that money, but those agents haven't come up with anything that's right. Course, my needs are a bit particular. I need a big place with a triple garage, a large room for parties and a private sun-terrace...see, I like to sunbathe in the nude. One doesn't want to feel frustrated when the sun comes out, does one?' The only small cloud on that sunny horizon was quite how to utilize his snowballing income for, as Lionel confessed, 'I've lost count of how much money I'm making.'

Others had not. The sixteen numbers from *Oliver!* had just been knocked down to New York publisher Howie Richman for over $40,000 (£15,000) – reputedly a fatter cheque than Rodgers and Hammerstein received from some of their music rights in Britain. Plays had been sold to the States before, but no one in the music business could remember when a show had pulled in such a huge advance, fully nine months before any projected Broadway run. And not just any Broadway producer was in the bidding. It was all down to David Merrick, undisputed king of the Great White Way. The reason, according to Bart, was a hunger for something to amuse the Americans' jaded tastebuds. He had just spent two weeks in New York, and reported back that all the stage shows (with the exception of *West Side Story*, which had been running there since 26 September 1957) were presented to a formula unchanged since *Oklahoma!* 'They are ready for something fresh in style. I was worried about *Oliver!* at first, but at least it is fresh. I also think it's important for a musical to say something. It must be entertainment first, but that's not enough. I believe *Oliver!* is a success because it is really the story of a

49

little boy's search for love – and that's what everyone is looking for.'

Bygraves also had a theory. 'For the first time in years, somebody is really writing British. We have been overfed with American music – and so have the Americans. Bart has pulled off a hit British musical, and even the British are surprised.' Added to which was the interest being shown in the production by visiting American theatregoers, who were trudging up the stairs of Lakeview Music in London's Tin Pan Alley, mistakenly assuming it was a music store where they could purchase the score. Others were smuggling the LP back into the States, just as the discs of *My Fair Lady* had been smuggled into London while the show was basking on Broadway.

And yet...and yet. The question was being asked: was it all really Lionel's own work?[8] It is a rare combination: the musical talent to write a score, the dramatic inspiration to produce a tense narrative book, and the wit to convey emotion through lyrics. Bart repeatedly makes the point that he was the first to do so in any degree.

Only a fortnight after *Oliver!*'s triumphal first night, Lionel was in the witness box in a complicated case of publishing rights: John Kennedy and Larry Parnes were suing the *Weekly Sporting Review and Show Business* (the edition at issue had appeared on 22 March 1957) over credits to songs written, or co-written, by Bart and others. Lionel was asked by counsel for the defence, Mr Helenus Milmo, why the song 'Pretty Daisy', written for Tommy Steele together with fellow Cavemen Steele and Mike Pratt in August 1956, was also credited on the publishing details as being further co-authored by Messrs Wright and Tuvey. Bart explained succinctly that it had 'something to do with the Performing Right Society' and that he received a small cheque as his cut on advance royalties. 'When we wrote Tommy's first hit song "Rock With the Caveman", Frank Chacksfield was listed on the contract as one of the composers, so that he could get his cut of one quarter.'

And less than a year after *Oliver!* opened he was being sued over a copyright technicality. The Denmark Street music publisher Peter Maurice alleged that Bart wrote the show's songs while under contract to his company, and that the songs were therefore its property. Bart dismissed it all as 'a nonsensical claim. Naturally I am defending it. There are sixteen songs in

Oliver! and I think they are alleging half are theirs.' The Peter Maurice Music Company also made an application, heard by Mr Justice Buckley on 9 June 1961, for an interlocutory order directing that half the proceeds of *Oliver!* be frozen and that an injunction be issued restraining the defendants (Bart himself, Lakeview Music and Donmar Productions Ltd) from granting any rights in respect of the show without notice to Maurice's solicitors. At the hearing, Mr Guy Aldous, QC, for the plaintiffs, said that Bart had written the music and lyrics of *Oliver!* between March 1957 and February 1959, while in the plaintiffs' employ under contract. In an affidavit, Bart stated that when he began working for the plaintiffs, he was principally engaged in writing 'hits', and that indeed he had even tried to interest the music firm in the musical, only to be told by managing director James Phillips: 'All that show business is all right for your own amusement, but why don't you sit down and write a hit song for Tommy Steele?' The judge refused to grant an interim order, and did not think that, pending the trial, he should interfere with the defendants' financial business arrangements by sterilizing part of the show's receipts. That must have come as some small relief to Lionel, who was at that very moment spending some of the show's receipts in the South of France. He was informed of the outcome by telegram... while sunbathing.

CHAPTER FIVE

OOM-PAH-PAH

In the closing days of 1961, Lionel woke up to the morning noises of his mews flat. From his first-floor living-room he could see a bedraggled man with a Peter Sellers moustache, playing 'Mary's Boy Child' on a battered silver cornet. Out on the Fulham Road a bereted Breton on a bicycle was peddling 'Oignons!' And the antique fellow who owned a harp shop around the corner was complaining about a locked car parked in front of his garage. In the distance a delivery boy may well have been cycling along, humming Bart's latest pop record 'Give Us a Kiss for Christmas'. This irritatingly catchy ditty had been written for Tommy Steele, but when he was unavailable to record the novelty record in time for a pre-Christmas release, Decca allowed Bart to cut it himself, with a children's chorus coming in at the end, and two loud kisses to finish things off on the right note.

There was another, more persistent noise that morning, as well. A loud buzzing in Mr Bart's head to remind him of his 'fab' previous night. Noël Coward had visited Reece Mews to listen to a tape of Bart's new musical *Blitz!* The Master talked and talked, as the glasses chinked and were constantly refilled. Coward was Bart's new-found mentor, hero, uncle, friend, sophisticate and, most usefully, confidant in matters amorous

and glamorous. One year earlier, on 20 October 1960, 'behind the dark-
est pair of dark glasses seen for a long time at London Airport' (as the
Evening Standard reported it), Lionel had flown off to Geneva for his first
meeting with the lugubrious-looking songwriter and 'wit'. It was a
long-awaited weekend house-party; not many weeks before, Li had
been on a trip to Paris with Judy Garland,[1] where they met their mutual
friends Terence Rattigan and Maggie Leighton, who engineered an
introduction to Coward. The Master had already sent Bart a fan
telegram after seeing *Oliver!*, with the high praise that Bart was the
greatest English composer since himself. Encouraged and inspired, Bart
took the opportunity of seeking further approval for *Blitz!* among a raft
of other, less assured projects like the French bedroom farce musical
about Napoleon and Josephine for Anthony Newley and Shirley Bassey.
In a more dignified version, perhaps, of you-show-me-yours, the older
composer asked Lionel's opinion of a new musical *he* was completing.
Bart came away from the weekend elated and clutching the gift Noël
had presented to him – a rhyming dictionary, with the dedication: 'Do
not let this aid to rhyming/Bitch your talent and your timing'.[2]

Seeing Noël and Coley[3] and the way they lived at their mountain
hideaway gave Li a taste for more gracious living. He too now wanted a
villa (though he wanted his in the south of France), a penthouse in New
York and a town house in London. The only thing lacking in this lush,
gorgeous life that musicals could offer him was the chance to share it
with someone. 'It's success as a human being what matters. And I don't
feel I'm a success at that...it's like I feel I'm missing out on something...I
don't quite know what...security, I guess. Emotional security. Emotional
security of one person depends on another person, and let's say I haven't
found that other person.' Coward, by contrast, had. His love life was as
stable as an ocean liner, while Bart was skipper of a flimsy craft tossed
this way and that by all the jetsam that passed by and momentarily clung
to the superstructure.

Following the nose job, Lionel had begun to work on the inner man
– cultivating the mannerisms (including an intermittent Churchillian
lisp), polishing the affectations, refining the Cockney twang into a hep-cat
dialect rather than a gor-blimey embarrassment. Celebrity and fame

inevitably require a ready-to-wear public face, and Lionel always kept his abreast of fashion, mixing with the right 'in' names, fostering the goodwill of the likeliest up-and-coming.

A new year was about to begin, and with it a new amusement to stave off boredom. Michael Codron[4] and Lionel together formed the Playwright Producer's Guild, whose aim was to further the development of new talent in the theatre. Their first project would be *Why the Chicken?* by the unknown twenty-four-year-old John McGrath, a story of rebellious teenagers transplanted from over-populated inner cities to a new town. Bart was to write incidental music, a theme song, and also direct. Sean Kenny was designing the sets, with a West End run forecast. Rehearsals[5] began in a hall in Bloomsbury in February of 1961 – interrupted only briefly that month when Lionel collected his Variety Club Award as Show Business Personality of 1960, the same year that fifteen-year-old Hayley Mills was best film actress, Peter Sellers best film actor and Albert Finney the Most Promising Newcomer.

In the middle of that same month Columbia Records released the title single 'Why the Chicken?', which was the first song published by Lionel's new company Apollo Music Ltd. In the middle of the following month Lionel was told that his first attempt at stage directing was not going to transfer to the West End. After trial runs at Wimbledon, Streatham and Golders Green, the cast were given notice following the Saturday night performance at the Golders Green Hippodrome at the end of March. Lionel told them he was going away for a couple of weeks, but that when he returned he planned to take the play on a provincial tour. But, according to a spokesman for the producing company, 'There are no further bookings.'

Lionel had an apostolic belief that the play would be an irresistible lure for the disaffected youth of Britain, and lamented the dreary audiences who were the mainstay of the West End, those for whom most of the traditional West End product was written. The first night was to have been quite something. 'I want as many of my mates there as possible – all the rock 'n' roll kids like Tommy and Adam and Cliff. That is to say, it will be the usual type of première plus the teenage element.' And maybe it would have been...

Apollo Music, on the other hand, was very much in the business. It had already provided Bart with a chauffeur-driven Rolls-Royce. Its offices were carpeted wall-to-wall in olive green deep-pile Axminster. Interior decorators had transformed a neglected shell into a monument to Bart's rickety taste: built-in television and stereo, a very grand piano and an illuminated portrait of the publisher himself, hanging in a gilt-edged frame. 'It will be the most luscious music publishers in London. The whole thing is Greek, you see – Apollo. When it's finished, I'll throw a ball.' And well he might, in order to reduce some of his taxable income. The premises were reckoned to have cost £10,000 to renovate, plus a further £2,500 to equip, plus the salaries of a general manager, Leslie Paul, and other staff. Yet, Lionel calculated that 'Living Doll' alone had made him £11,000–£12,000. He currently had 8 per cent of the gross of *Oliver!*, which was taking between £8,000–£9,000 a week, to say nothing of a 2 per cent gross from *Fings*. Something in excess of £1,000 each week was pouring into his coffers, not taking into account his fees from recordings, and all the little et ceteras that kept his accountants happy.

But the Apollo Music Company also had philanthropic aspirations; at least, its president had. 'What I will do is contract two or three young writers, and I will go in on Fridays and see what they've been doing during the week. I want to establish a couple of other faces. Rock 'n' roll isn't dead, you know. Kids always want beat music they can dance to. It must be exciting and it must have intrigue value. Bobby Darin and John Barry[6] are the people who point the way to the teenage stuff in the years to come. They aren't writing down to the kids.'

At the beginning of July 1961 the 'in-crowd' of London squeezed into their turtle necks and Chelsea boots for the party which was to launch this venture. *'I'm giving a tiny cocktail party'* ran the stencilled invitation on the right people's mantelpieces. It was signed with a brush pen and immense flourish in letters two inches high – *Li*. The tiny 'do' was also to celebrate the fact that Marty Wilde had at last recorded a song of Lionel's – 'Hide and Seek', released on the Philips label in the stripy white-and-blue paper sleeves. The first song Bart had written for Marty, 'Happiness', had been turned down by the quiffed heart-throb, and

Lionel was in no mood to be reminded of the fact at his own bash. 'We went cool on it. Maybe he didn't like my demonstration disc. You see, I work like this. When I write a song, I stand in front of the mirror and do an impersonation of the person the song is for. I do all their movements and everything. Then I make this rather dodgy demo record in the style of the artiste. I have my Lonnie voice, my Cliff voice, my Marty voice. This song is my best hit potential since "Living Doll". As for Marty, I was so impressed with him in *Bye Bye Birdie* that I want to do a show round him. Marty is entrenching himself in the ranks of the performers of England – I would put him among the first ten. He has this magnetic quality.' Despite Bart's enthusiasm and despite the party atmosphere in Shaftesbury Avenue that evening, Marty was somewhat moody and began confessing that, whatever Lionel's opinion, he didn't like his own recording of 'Hide and Seek'. 'It's mainly myself I'm displeased with. I'm a perfectionist. Mr Bart is a good songwriter.'

Also at the party, though not yet in the foreground, was a seventeen-year-old office-boy, who had recently been promoted to singing the company's demo discs...until he decided that he was good enough to make the finished recordings and have his own name on the labels. His name was Robert Farrant, though not for very long. Bart also thought the boy had talent and, in the fashion of Larry Parnes, made him become Bobby Shaftoe. 'I was never mad about it. In fact, I was embarrassed by it. But you just accepted that it was the thing to do...no questions asked.' Lionel wrote the Bobby Shaftoe hit 'Over and Over', which was recorded by Parlophone and led to engagements on tour with Dusty Springfield, Gerry and the Pacemakers and Billy J Kramer. 'Then I remember one day on stage in Chester-le-Street, I was literally trying to compete with the bingo-caller, and decided it was time to ship Bobby Shaftoe out to sea. I'd also seen too much of the scene – the drink and the drugs – and I would have been dead by now if I'd got too deep into that. But I'm still grateful to Lionel for getting me started in the business – he's a great ideas man. The only trouble with Lionel was that he enjoyed playing the role of Lionel Bart too much.'

Whether or not he was always a *good* songwriter, Bart was nevertheless maintaining his record as Britain's most *prolific* tunesmith. He was putting some finishing flourishes to *Blitz!*, a wartime nostalgia musical to rival Coward's *Cavalcade*, with more songs – twenty-seven in all – even than *Oliver!* The entire project was destined to be on an epic scale: a cast of sixty or seventy would be required to populate war-torn London; Sean Kenny's sets had to recreate such landmarks as Victoria Station and the Underground; a production budget of at least £100,000 was talked about. Kenny had built a mock-up of the immense scenery in a space above Peter Cook's Establishment Club in Greek Street, Soho. Bart planned to use devices that had never before been used in the theatre – film projected on to dry ice which dissolved to clear the way for the next scene, radio-controlled sets that moved into place on the stage without the need for dozens of costly stagehands (on double- and triple-time every evening, thanks to the punitive union stranglehold on the West End). And yet it was this very ambition to be bigger and better than *Cavalcade* that ruled out a provincial try-out tour. The £40,000 cement and steel sets were never going to be portable, and the scale of the production was causing further technical problems: there were few theatres with the dimensions or the backstage and fly-tower area required to house the revolving sets, and twenty outer-London cinemas were looked at before a flat-bed stage could be found (at the 1,200-seat Regal, Edmonton) for a pre-West End run of the maximum allowable twenty-one previews.

It was to be part of Bart's crusade against timid theatre managements who, according to the go-ahead one-man musical dynamo, were holding theatre back from its rightful inheritance. England at the time, of course, had a theatrical industry governed by two or three all-powerful producers, and a theatrical product which was subject to the blue-pencil scrutiny of the Lord Chamberlain's team of avid censors. In the 'Mark My Words' column in the long-defunct magazine *Today*, Bart took the opportunity to give his timid enemies a caning:

The theatre in England today is convalescing. It has been a little ill. In fact, some of the illness remains. The complaint is a simple one. The theatre is so buried in tradition that many managements are still living in Edwardian times, and they still believe that a play has to have a star

57

gentleman and a star lady. The poor management...what is there left, when one has run through the stock of classical plays containing tailor-made parts for one's stable of dames and knights?

Should one look again towards Broadway and import a ready-made American success in the hope that this will have a London success? Unfortunately in the last year or so this measure has not proved very profitable. I think that theatre managements must learn that the audiences of 1960 are more aware than they were twenty years ago; and that they do not expect the same old stuff. They do not respect star names as much as they respect truth. The audiences of today wish to be involved and not spoken down to from a great distance as in the drawing-room class comedy or imported French translations of these, where the only audience involvement is the drilled applause on the entrance and exit of the stars.

So should one perhaps dare to originate a British production with no star names, from an author or composer with perhaps no reputation? I'm afraid the desire in most of these managements to become a ripple on the new wave is dampened by the more urgent desire to remain safe in the lap of tradition. How safe? How long will it be before Drury Lane presents a British musical? It is not that I have any objections to them presenting an American musical if it is one like *West Side Story* which – let's face it – is the only large-scaled American musical to break from the brash formula of *Oklahoma!* since that momentous opening in the New York Guild some nineteen long years ago.

I'm not of course against using established stars, either, provided they are cast with some sense of truth. Just as audiences want more and more to be involved with the story from the standpoint of our feelings and experience in this age, they are mostly looking for truth in casting today. I'm pleased to see that there's been some progress from the day two years ago when I hawked *Oliver!* around to various managements, one of whom thought it was too dreary a subject and needed a gimmick. This particular gentleman suggested in all seriousness that we should consider using an all-black cast. At this point I had seriously to consider his suggestion.

And I can now call my new musical *Blitz!*, instead of *Strolling Down the Lane* as a certain traditional management suggested. Now *Blitz!* is true and real and is a title created by and belonging to the people of London. *Strolling Down the Lane* – that's what Edwardian managements think that the people of London would like. Therein is the illness, and, I hope, my contribution towards the cure.

'Heart, Guts and Truth' was how Bart was modestly describing his forthcoming extravaganza, which (like *Oliver!*) was being presented by Donald Albery. Opening night was under threat from a proposed Musicians' Union strike, but was nevertheless scheduled for 8 May 1962, the seventeenth anniversary of VE Day, a coincidence Bart was willing to put down simply to 'showmanship', a commodity he was rarely lacking in the sixties. He was also telling anyone who'd listen that this was going to be 'the biggest and most expensive musical show to originate in this country', though why he should have thought this would be an advantage is, in hindsight, difficult to imagine. A further supposed advantage was the engagement of the author/composer/lyricist as director, with a little help from Eleanor 'Fizz' Fazan (producer of *Beyond the Fringe*) and dance director Teddy Green, who had received high praise when he choreographed *The Young Ones* for Cliff. According to Bart, the reasons for appointing himself were twofold: no director who was interested in the project was available until late the following year; and, more importantly, 'This is a British show about the East End of London during the Blitz. In a way it's about me. I was an evacuee then, but returned to London on several occasions, curiously enough when bombing was most severe. I am writing *Blitz!* from a child's-eye view of it. I have talked to old-age pensioners, read scores of letters from people with air-raid stories to tell – characteristically, most of them are humorous – and much of my time is spent with well-known wartime personalities. The show is also about intolerance and the effect of the 1941 bombings on East End Jews and Cockneys.' In fact, Bart claimed that it was as much an attempt to follow Vaughan Williams[7] and that, ten years earlier, he had actually begun a project to record all the songs and sounds of Petticoat Lane before they disappeared. 'I've gone back to English folk groups and based things on English street cries and English nursery rhymes. And I'm a Jew, so there are Jewish things in it, too. I use jazz where it comes in. Jazz is unavoidable; it means today, 1962; it means civilization or decadence, whichever is the right word. I'm not a musical scholar but I have a good ear and I've gone into musical origins. Jazz, real African jazz, isn't far from Jewish music, which is quite close to Gregorian, and leads on to Celtic music and then to English folk songs and Cockney street chants.

'In *Blitz!* I have tried to isolate music which is period pastiche from music which is dramatic statement. There is period pastiche to create the atmosphere of those days, but the dramatic statement is my own, and timeless. I may use something which has the feeling of "We'll Hang Out the Washing on the Siegfried Line" to convey atmosphere, but the lovers' duet relating to a dramatic mood is musically 1962 because that's as far advanced as I go.'

When it came to casting, Lionel also insisted on the personal touch, and told the *Daily Mail* that he wanted a twenty-five-year-old fairground barker to take the leading role of Georgie Locke, a teenage Cockney soldier. His name was Doug Sheldon, and his career had begun running bingo sessions and donkey derbies in his father's amusement park at Skegness. He had come to Lionel's attention as the blond, blue-eyed six-footer (according to Doug, he was descended from a ninth-century Viking visitor to Britain) who had just recorded a hit single 'Runaround Sue' and had had a bit part in the film *The Guns of Navarone.* 'I've seen Sheldon act and I've heard him sing, and this boy can really wail. I want him for the part. It's a tough role – seven songs – and there are only two or three people I know who could get anywhere near it. He can not only sing and act, he looks the part as well.' One of those six-foot-tall, blue-eyed, fair-haired Viking Cockneys, as the *Mail's* uncharitably cynical journalist noted. Sadly, Mr Sheldon is not credited with the part of Georgie Locke in the programme for *Blitz!* (instead, it went to Graham James).

In spite of the personal associations and inspiration, Bart again turned to Joan Maitland, his long-serving personal assistant and sounding-board, as co-writer of the book.[8] Their story is the *Mother Courage* saga of Mrs

Blitzstein, a part which was originally conceived for Tessie O'Shea or Rita Webb, but which went to Amelia Bayntun, whose £200-a-week pay packet from the show was probably four times what her husband was earning as landlord of the Grapes pub in Regent Street. She played the Yiddisher momma who runs a pickled-herring stall. Her daughter falls for Georgie the goy next door (his dad is, conveniently, a cloth-capped, pipe-smoking Cockney stereotype continually exposing his waistline, his tattoos and his miserable anti-Semitic prejudices), and her prodigal son has a sub-plot almost entirely to himself. But the tale of thwarted love dodging Hitler's Luftwaffe was seen by some as little better than a kit-assembled vehicle for a few good songs and a couple of bad ones. Despite the voices of Lionel Gamlin reading the BBC news, of Winston Churchill and of Vera Lynn (heard only off-stage), and despite a couple of tunes that show Lionel at his breezy best ('Mums and Dads' and 'Who's This Geezer Hitler?'), there is an underlying mawkishness and banality to the lyrics and the characterizations. And the theme *was* somewhat similar to *West Side Story* – or even that show's venerable ancestor, *Romeo and Juliet*. By the time of the first previews, the show had become dangerously unwieldy: a cast of fifty-seven, an orchestra of ninety and a running-time of three hours plus. Lionel, with four hours' sleep a night and a hundred cigarettes a day, was on top of it, however. 'Oh, I know what's wrong with it. Too much chat. Got to keep the action going. And I've got to write another couple of songs. That's for sure.'

If Bart read the first reviews, he would have heard the same misgivings repeated back to him several-fold. First the *Mirror*, in which Donald Zec carped: 'The jokes fell thick and slow, spluttering like dud incendiaries...But for me – a near miss.' The *Express* began by reviewing the audience: 'It started at 7.10 last night, and was all over at 9.55. The applause was rapturous. The curtain leaped up and down like a camera shutter. The cast lined up on stage and sang all the songs they hope the entire country will be singing in the months to come.' But the Voice of Britain then went on to warn us that 'first night reactions are notoriously misleading, being motivated by uncritical sentiment and good will so thick you can practically feel it sharing your seat. And so it remains to be said – after the monstrous build-up and the months of brouhaha – that Lionel Bart's *Blitz!* while not a failure, is a massive disappointment and, for at least half its length, a bore.' Bernard Levin had more serious misgivings about the sub-plot. Mama Blitzstein's son, Harry, is pictured as a deserter and a black marketeer whose companion is a flashy West Indian, which leads Levin to accuse Bart of 'a piece of uncharitable tastelessness at the expense of representatives of two minority racial groups that is doubly surprising considering its source'. Mr Levin himself is more charitable in conclusion, when he anoints Bart 'the best song-writer in the country'.

The one element that might save the show from instant oblivion, according to *The Times*,[9] was 'a stage set of quite staggering magnificence...which in the opening scene soars up to the flies disclosing an Underground station in which the cast are bedding themselves down during an air raid...the production launches into ferociously life-like replicas of the bombing. Fires burst out in back-projection; masonry crashes across the luridly darkened stage...' Only the veteran W. A. Darlington in the *Telegraph* allowed himself a little incautious excitement. For him, *Blitz!* 'is going to be a whacking, walloping hit. Furthermore, I should offer, if it doesn't turn out that way, to eat my oldest hat. I can hardly imagine a less palatable meal.'

If only Bart had chosen to read nothing but the *Daily Telegraph* on the morning of 9 May 1962. At one in the afternoon, wearing a light-green peaked *Oliver!* hat, light-green man-made-fibre suit, navy shirt stitched with white (no tie), navy paisley silk handkerchief and navy suede shoes, he sipped a soft drink ('It's too early in my day to start drinking') and told the *Evening Standard*, 'I didn't read them before I went to bed at 5 a.m., because I wanted to be sure of a few hours' peaceful sleep. To be honest, I was a little upset at first. Not because some critics had panned the show but because some had overlooked the main adventure of the piece, and hadn't seen what I was getting at. I may be a baby but I have had three or four first nights, and I think *Blitz!* is an absolute storm. I don't want to make an enemy of the critics, or be their friend, but I think a few of them were out to get me. After all, continual success makes very dull copy. But the box office is what matters, and I've just had a call that bookings are double those of yesterday.' Mercifully, those bookings were made a few days before Ken Tynan skewered his pen into the show in Sunday morning's *Observer*. 'On the whole, it would have been a better idea if Lionel Bart had written a sequel to *Oliver!* about modern youth and called it *Twist!* Mawkish where it tries to be poignant, flat where it means to be funny, and second-hand where it aims at period authenticity, *Blitz!* is a misfire on a grand scale, despite the devoted salvage work of Amelia Bayntun and a supporting cast of between twenty-eight and ninety-seven players. (Amid so much smoke, it is hard to be sure.)' And the salvos do not stop there. Tynan rallies, with a veiled accusation of plagiarism. 'The songs are straightforward music-hall stuff, spiced now and then with hints that the composer-lyricist is aware, if only tele-pathically, of the achievements of composers whose work is less well known in England than his own; by a sort of osmosis, phrases and cadences from minor American musicals seep into his melodies; and there is one tune – a lively children's number called "Mums and Dads" – that sounds exactly like a reject from *Oliver!*'

And there were more than mere hints at plagiarism from at least one quarter. In a paragraph following Bernard Levin's notice in the *Daily Express* was the following news-in-brief: 'A legal row burst over *Blitz!* last night. Alex Murray, twenty-two-year-old pop singer, claimed he helped write some of the tunes. He said: "I am considering legal action." Mr Bart's solicitor said: "Mr Bart is the sole author of the words and music and the songs."' Even curiouser: in the same paper, one week later, appears the headline 'BART TO SUE OVER BLITZ!' above this story: 'Lionel Bart, author of the West End musical *Blitz!* is suing music-arranger Bob Sharples. It is understood Mr Bart wants a judgment that he wrote all the music for the show. Mr Sharples's solicitor said yester-day: "The action will be strenuously defended." Mr Sharples is himself suing Donmar Productions – which presents *Blitz!* – claiming he com-posed some music in the show.' It was perhaps tempting providence when, in *The Times* a couple of months before the opening, Lionel had announced: 'I've made the orchestrations, although I've not written down the dots...First I made a tape of the entire score, singing some of it myself and with other singers to help, with a small group – piano, bass and strings – to accompany. We've gone on from there, and fortunately there's a very good *rapport* between Bob Sharples and me. We get the rhythm and pointing I need. Then we get the harmony. Then we go on to the texture. If we don't get it right, we scrap it and start again. That may be an expensive method but we've found that it works.'[10]

Blitz! began its run at the Adelphi, on the Strand, on 8 May 1962, and stayed there until 14 September 1963. It was the same theatre that was to house Bart's next stage musical in September 1964. But he was not a man to stand still in the swinging sixties. In 1961 there had been talk of a show to be specially written for Sammy Davis, Jr, who was over then for a seven-week cabaret season at the Prince of Wales. In September that same year Lionel had attended the Swedish première of *Oliver!* This, though, was hardly the success that London was witnessing. The Swedish stage rights were owned by Lars Schmidt, whose wife, Mrs Schmidt, was to many more familiar as Ingrid Bergman. *Oliver!* was to open the new season at Stockholm's Oscars Theatre, following on from *My Fair Lady*, which had broken all box-office records there. Jarl Kulle, who had played Higgins, was now Fagin, but the production as a whole was dismissed as 'poor and unengaging', leaving the first nighters unmistakably disappointed. Still, the very next week Lionel was in perkier mood following news from Melbourne: Sir Frank Tait's production company had opened *Oliver!* there to overwhelming acclaim. The cable reached Bart at a health hydro, where the 'over-tired' composer had been shedding two pounds (and resting his duodenal ulcer) alongside some doughty dowagers. Back in London, the supply of little angels to the show had all but dried up, and the search was on again for cherubic boys over twelve and under 4 foot 10 inches with good voices. The production was half way through its second year, and had got through six Olivers already because of the law forbidding any boy from playing the part for more than thirty weeks, with an understudy required every ten weeks to allow the principal some time off. Apparently, it was easy enough to find actors who could play the 'less cultivated boys', but angels were harder to come by.

For Bart, now reported to be earning 'something like £50,000 a year', it was also time for another holiday, and the search for winter sun

took him to Majorca. It was noted by the press that he flew out and flew
back on the same day as Alma Cogan, to which Bart's gnomic reply was
'Just coincidence'. In fact, his bachelorhood was already a subject for the
speculators who like to see every showbusiness name linked with
another. In an outlandish two-paragraph story in the *Express* at the end
of 1962, when Bart was in America for two months, William Hickey's
readers were solemnly informed that 'Judy Garland and Lionel Bart have
been seen together in New York so much that columnists are hinting at
a wedding when Judy is free of her marriage to Sid Luft. But Bart told
me today: "We have known each other a long time. Marriage? No. We
are just permanent friends."'

With *Blitz!* barely three months into its run, Lionel had some news to
communicate to the press. A new musical, 'very much bigger even than
Blitz!' was announced at the end of August 1962. The show was to be
based on the story of *The Hunchback of Notre Dame*. Lionel announced
that he had been working on it for four weeks, and expected to complete it in about another four. Every line of dialogue was to be sung by
up to a hundred voices – no orchestra.

Only five days earlier Bart had returned from supervising *Oliver!* at
the Los Angeles Philharmonic Auditorium, where it was to have a
seven-week run as the highlight of the twenty-fifth anniversary season
of the Los Angeles Civic Light Opera Association. With perhaps with a
little too much frankness, he admitted there was nothing for him to do
over there 'except be a playboy...although I met some swinging people –
Groucho Marx and Sal Mineo'. And he was naturally eager to tell the
waiting world exactly how he had come by the idea for the slowest-
burning fuse of his life – one that has still failed to ignite any pyrotech-
nic. Inspiration, it appears, had struck in a menswear shop in New York.
Lionel was trying on a turtle-neck sweater and, with his head stuck
firmly inside the opening, thought, 'Blimey! It makes me look like the
hunchback of Notre Dame.' In a no doubt unintentional pun, he went
on: 'Then all the bells started ringing, and I knew I'd got it – the idea for
another show.' Bart claims he shocked the salesman by running out of
the shop, shouting at the top of his voice, 'I've got it. I've got it at last.'
He did not buy the pullover. If he had, it might serve to remind him

today of the burden he has shouldered ever since. That day in August, however, he was brimful of enthusiasm and bluster. 'It's a natural. Can't think why nobody thought of it before. I'm writing it as a "quickie". Should have the first draft done in a couple of weeks...music, songs, book and all. Maybe I'll present it first in America. I've got three shows in London now, and if I had a fourth I'd be competing for audiences against myself.'

Not the issue that was worrying *The Times*. In a leader on 8 September 1962, the journal of record pondered the change that had come about in the musical comedy, once 'an easy-going, romantic, sentimental form of entertainment...committed to careful avoidance of the disturbing, the intellectual, or the less than completely pleasant'. The editorial goes on to suppose that a new intellectualism is abroad in the form, forcing composers to turn to novels rather than to plays for their raw material, and hinting that only a few years earlier, surprise might have been expressed at Bart's choice of Victor Hugo...or even Dickens. In conclusion: 'It is natural that not every lover of nineteenth-century literature will find himself completely happy about its conversion into a twentieth-century form.'

Difficult questions were also being asked about the originality of some of Lionel's songs. Accusations were commonly expressed that Lionel Bart was a derivative composer, with 'Fings' often being compared to 'Mountain Greenery'. Unshaken, Lionel always gave the same reply. 'People like what's familiar. They're thinking a note ahead every time they hear a tune, a word ahead when they listen to a lyric. All I do is to let them feel both are familiar, recognized...then give them a little surprise by changing a phrase.' And, as if he felt the need to reinforce his case, he took to publicizing (in the hammiest manner imaginable) the very secrets of his enviable success. 'I do most of my work in restaurants. I get terrific ideas while I am eating, so I scribble the whole thing down on the paper napkins, and stuff them into my pockets. Sometimes I go mad trying to find one in trousers sent to the cleaners.' Then, to demonstrate the formula, Bart whips out his pocket tape-recorder over steak and chips in a Soho restaurant, and starts to sing into it! 'Just an idea for a song.' It was a simple formula, simply executed by lah-lahing into the portable, or into the microphone of a brand-new Japanese stereo reel-to-reel that had cost the musically illiterate composer just over £400. And that's all it took for him to win three Tony awards in 1963,[11] when *Oliver!* won best composer and lyricist for Bart, best scenic designer for Sean Kenny and best conductor for Donald Pippin.

Broadway had bought Bart wholesale, and for the £7,000-a-week songsmith it was a two-way love affair. As with any affair, there were difficult moments: 'In the US, you get about twenty-five show doctors coming in, saying, "Where are the girls?" It took nine years to get *West Side Story* on. They lack adventure over there.' Notwithstanding all that, *Fings* was due to open in September. *Quasimodo* was, according to Bart in May 1963, 'now finished' and due to open there in the spring of '64. He had been asked to write the music for a film of Stephen Mead's novel *How to Succeed With Women Without Really Trying*. There was the Broadway commission for a musical of *Cyrano de Bergerac* with Peter O'Toole. A $1,500,000 offer had been made for the movie rights to *Blitz!*, and the stage show was reputedly going to be the most expensive ever seen in New York, costing at least £262,000 – more than twice the average for a full-scale musical. But what could the Broadway backers lose? Bart was on a roll. *Blitz!* was due to close in London on 14 September after an eighteen-month run, which had repaid the show's £60,000 costs in the first four months. In that Kennedy assassination year alone, Bart made at least half a dozen transatlantic journeys – not with the economy or comfort we expect today: TWA's twenty-one-day fare from London to New York was £125 while, for only an additional £13, the *Queen Mary* offered a single first-class cabin from New York to Southampton. A BOAC-liveried Lockheed Constellation might have taken twelve noisy if pressurized hours to complete the crossing – it mattered little to Lionel, who returned with a trunkful of trophies after each trip: snake-skin Texan cowboy boots one time, a *Bonanza*-sized stetson another. And on one occasion, a friendship with Richard Rodgers. The veteran had three shows on in London himself that year, including *No Strings* and *Boys From Syracuse*, and was reputedly looking for a collaborator to replace Lorenz Hart and Oscar Hammerstein. But, when asked about the possibility of a Bart instead of a Hart, Rodgers made a cryptic remark: 'My next partner must bring ideas and high ability with him, not just friendship.'

The year ended with Lionel in the bosom of old friends from his Theatre Workshop days – in panto. *The Merry Rooster's Panto* was the West End's only traditional Christmas entertainment that season, and was to run matinées only at the Wyndham's, where *Oh! What a Lovely War* was playing in the evenings. Joan Littlewood brought together Peter Shaffer and Steven Vinaver on the script, with Lionel and Stanley Myers providing the songs. Barbara Ferris was to play Cindy, with Victor Spinetti and Brian Murphy as the Ugly Sisters. And Tommy Steele's wife Ann Donoghue returned to the stage in several parts – the first time she had acted since her marriage.

Bart's musicals were beginning to have a consistent theme: champion the underdog. As in Anthony Newley's *Stop the World, I Want to Get Off*, which had opened at the Queen's Theatre in the summer of 1961, there was always a role for the Little Man, the one who didn't want to be, but invariably would be, pushed around. Nevertheless, the soon-to-be millionaire tailor's boy denied that he had any political axes to grind, and shied away from the left-wing musical that he was regularly expected to produce. 'Despite my early days with Unity Theatre when I worked with Alfie Bass in a number of effective political revues, I feel I'm not the kind of man now to hammer home politics from a soap-box. But I have toyed with ideas of a Socialist nature. A musical – or, better still, a film – based on the Ban-the-Bomb campaign could be a world beater. It could be set within the format of *The Canterbury Tales* with Aldermaston marchers and traditional jazz bands visiting pubs and squares.'

Nevertheless, in spite of these denials, his next major work for the theatre was imbued with red. Lionel called it 'a folk opera set in Liverpool'. The sixties in that sprawling north-western port marked the end of traditional dock work and the dawn of a charmed era in which Liverpool, and in particular its Cavern Club, became the birthplace of a Mersey sound that gave us Gerry and the Pacemakers, Cilla Black and the Beatles themselves. The city has an anarchic, self-mocking, almost self-destructive streak. Its landmark is the Liver Building, atop which roost the Liver Birds, and these have not only been incorporated into the city seal, they have hatched their own legends. According to Scouse nous, the male bird faces inland in order to see when the pub doors open, while the female looks out to sea to watch for the sailors coming ashore. It was this world that Lionel needed to capture in *Maggie May*.

'When we first got the idea for *Maggie May*, we were going to base it very loosely on the story of Mary Magdalen. We decided to set it in Liverpool docks, mainly because I wanted to bring the docks to life in the way that Gershwin did with New Orleans' Cat Fish Row in *Porgy and Bess*. So I went to live on Merseyside to pick up a feel for the music, and found that there was an Irish influence which made it very similar to the Jewish music that I knew so well.'

Bart, however, did not know the Scouse idiom so well that he could manage without a collaborator, and the story of how he came upon his co-author is fairly typical of the way he worked then and the way he still works now. A journalist, Leslie Mallory, from the *Daily Herald*, was interviewing Lionel a few days before Christmas in 1961. When they got round to talking about his future projects, the subject of the Liverpool 'folk opera' came up, and Lionel asked the journalist for suggestions: without much thought, he offered the best television playwright at the time Alun Owen, who went on to write *No Trams to Lime Street*. Before the words had dried on his lips, Bart was up like flash, snapping his fingers, shouting at his secretary ('pretty, dark-haired Muriel Matteoda') to 'Get him on the blower.' When the call was connected, she transferred it Lionel. 'Alun? Hello, Dad. Listen, I've got an idea. It's a gas. When can we meet? Tomorrow?' In three minutes they had formed a coherent plan. Any longer, and Bart might have tired of the idea, and moved on to the next one passing through his open window.

It is a colourful story, though it is not the one remembered three years later during a tense break in rehearsals three weeks before opening night. That version goes like this. *Maggie May* can be traced back to the night of 13 April 1962, the out-of-town opening of *Blitz!* in Edmonton, north London. The show had not gone well: the smoke effects went haywire. Bart was depressed, wanted to talk of other things. He walked to a café nearby with Georgia Brown, where they discussed Liverpool as

69

a setting for his next musical. He mentioned for the first time the ribald Merseyside ballad of 'Dirty Maggie May', which recounts how she picked up a sailor, did the business, then walked off with his pay packet while he slept it off. But Maggie, poor lass, was caught at it, and deported to Botany Bay.

> Oh dirty Maggie May
> They have taken her away,
> No more she'll walk down
> Lime Street after dark.

Bart next, so the story goes, telephoned Sean Kenny, who was immediately seduced by visions of a hard-edged dockside setting with its gaunt décor of steel girders and rivets. Then Kenny rang Alun Owen, the country's only Liverpool author, to arrange a meeting with Bart in the Establishment Club in Soho. Bart said simply 'Maggie May.' Owen agreed to write it. At the time, Bart had come up with no story-line, only an idea, and so a decision was taken to spend some time on Merseyside to soak up atmosphere. Owen told Bart: 'You've got to learn a whole new language. The Liverpool dialect, the real, *pure* Scouse is part-Irish, part-Welsh, part-catarrh.' In the pubs and on the docks they asked Liverpudlians to tell them about the legend of Maggie May. And, as with any folk legend, a number of versions turned up. For example, should the street song really be:

> My darlin' Maggie May
> They have taken her away
> She'll never walk down Lime Street any more.

> Judge and jury guilty found her
> Of robbing a homeward-bounder
> Now she'll never walk down Lime Street any more.

Once there, they found a city of 'All My Lovin'; they found Mabel's, a dockside pub where the jukebox pounded out 'Hold Your Hand'; they saw the mythical club, the Iron Door; they were taken into gambling dens where bundles were unrolled as the chemmy dealer flicked over the cards to the swish of fivers.

That original research period was followed by an enforced separation of six months while Lionel and Sean went to Broadway for the New York opening of *Oliver!*, leaving Alun behind to complete the outline of the book. He delivered them a three-hour script in which he had ignored what scant source material there was, and created a modern-day Maggie within a larger thematic story of strikes, dockers and male–female relationships.

'From there I just wrote the songs as it went along. Alun would often overwrite the script, so that I would have content for the lyrics in the songs to come. At that time I was very thick with Brian Epstein and all of the Beatles. They really took off in a big way as I was writing *Maggie May*, and John Lennon phoned me one day, saying, "Can I have a lend of your scriptwriter, we're going to do this film." So I downed tools for a couple of months, and Alun went off and wrote the screenplay for *A Hard Day's Night*.'

Whichever version of *Maggie May's* genesis you prefer, the collaboration fortuitously produced a reasonable show. The next job was casting. For a couple of years Bart had been doing his usual admirable job of self-publicity, and the names he bandied about for *Maggie* were hardly the ones that might be expected: the lead was written with Georgia Brown in mind as the tart with a heart, but she turned the role down. She was tired of her three-year run in *Oliver!*, both in the West End and on Broadway, and was not prepared for the same thing to be repeated. Not only that, she had established herself as a star in the States, and was unwilling to give that up. So would it go to Billie Whitelaw, who had appeared in several of Owen's plays? Meanwhile Peter O'Toole, according to Lionel, was ready and eager to play the docker! His film parts, however, might just prevent him being in it...so would it be Tom Bell instead? Auditions were even held to unearth raw talent in Liverpool itself, advertising for a voice that could belt out the blues, a big range, a glamorous spitfire with a very hard edge, aged between twenty-four and thirty. Little of any note emerged, except a letter from a lady who said that, though she couldn't sing much or act, *Maggie May* was the story of her life, and please note the above telephone number. Another contender stood up in a box at the audition theatre and declared, 'I don't want the job. I don't fancy any of them.' In the end, the adorable slag went to the most unlikely of interpreters. She was thirty-five, the daughter of a Welsh Baptist minister, and had not been in a West End musical since 1956, when she sang with O'Toole in the Bristol Old Vic production of *Oh, My Papa*. She did, though, have the good fortune to be married to Lionel's dear friend Rex Harrison. She auditioned, with piano accompaniment, and thus it was that the part went to Rachel Roberts. Her leading man was chosen more conventionally. Central to *Maggie* is the boyfriend, an easy-going docker called Joe Casey, who unwillingly has union leadership thrust upon him before a wildcat strike because of his father's heroic stand against the bosses a generation earlier. The initials are significant: just as Bart was comparing Maggie to Mary Magdalen, so Joe had a parallel in Jesus Christ. Despite this being his first appearance in a musical, the role went to Kenneth Haigh, a thirty-four-year-old who had created the original angry young man Jimmy Porter in John Osborne's *Look Back in Anger*. More recently, he had been Caligula in Camus' play of that name in London and New York – a necessary preparation for the bloodbath to come.

Further auditions brought in more than 200 hopeful beat groups. Owen and Bart wanted the 'authentic' Mersey sound, believing it to be essential to the musical's contemporary setting. Owen eventually went to his native Wales to find the Nocturnes, a Liverpool band earning £3–£5 a week each from playing in clubs. The line-up was: an estate agent's clerk, a butcher, a machine fitter, a labourer and a British Railways clerk. Better-known members of the company were John Junkin, from TV's *The Planemakers*, Michael Forrest of *Z-Cars*, and the Balladeer, who opens and closes proceedings as a story-teller, was Barry Humphries. As for a director, Jerome Robbins was at the top of Bart's list for a while, until the honour went to Ted Kotcheff, with fellow-Canadian Paddy Stone as choreographer. Bernard Delfont was to have sole rights as producer, the budget was to be £70,000, and an opening night was scheduled for 17 August 1964, at the Palace Theatre, Manchester. Why not

Liverpool? Simple: the set was once again enormous and made of steel sections, and the stage at the Empire could not handle it.

In fact, Sean Kenny's designs were to dog the show's progress throughout its workshop and rehearsal period. During the early part of the year, Kotcheff himself chose to spend time on Merseyside, getting a feel for the dialogue and the rhythm of work in the docks. Kenny was there, taking photos of the cranes and dock sheds. Everything was on a scale that made *Blitz!* look like a puppet show. He was tempted by the sight of a ship's bow as it was framed between the open ends of a warehouse. He noted the blues and reds of the drums on the quayside, waiting to be loaded. He imagined a scene as the New Brighton ferry sailed away from its berth.

When these visions were ultimately translated into stage sets, they weighed fifty tons, which meant that the stage at Manchester had to be reinforced for safety. Winches operating the huge sliding doors broke down regularly. Massively heavy steel dock-gates had to be scrapped and remade in aluminium. It was all beginning to worry the impresario Mr Delfont, who sat stony faced at the technical rehearsal, delayed by hitches. 'I hate mechanical effects. I don't like being at the mercy of a button. What happens if something breaks down? Still, there's something wrong with a musical if there isn't chaos before opening night. But it has to be organized chaos.'

It was hard, at that point, to know exactly who was doing the organizing. Bart had been rewriting music up to the last minute of dress rehearsals. His theatrical reputation was, after all, on the line following the tepid critical reaction to *Blitz!* At one point, in the closing hours at Manchester, twelve different versions of the last scene were under consideration. Bart, Alun Owen, Delfont, Kotcheff and Stone each had different ideas on how to bring down the final curtain. All five endings might be tried during the run, with the show closing differently every night. Bart was smoking five packs of cigarettes a day, and had taken to wearing wrap-around sunglasses constantly, even in the darkened theatre.

The first night, Bart had as his date Judy Garland, who subsequently recorded a handful of numbers from the show. As he remembers it,

Lionel and the cast drove over to Liverpool to celebrate, where Judy sang until morning in the Blue Angel Club. Before the end of the Manchester run, Bart himself was up on stage, standing in as the singing milkman for Fred Evans (also ballet master and lead dancer), who had been struck by tonsillitis. The tyro talent had two two-minute spots with a ditty entitled 'Shine, You Swine', and by all accounts acquitted himself well. But on the press night at the Adelphi he was on the stalls side of the safety curtain, wearing an eye-catching evening suit, designed by himself to be deliberately non-conformist, and made up for £60 by his tailor in Shepherd's Bush. In smooth, midnight-blue barathea, the suit had tighter than tight trousers and an eight-button jacket styled like an Edwardian tail-coat. On his feet, glistening patent-leather boots with Cuban heels, just one item from the twenty-five pairs of shoes, two pairs of cowboy boots, forty suits, forty shirts, dozens of hats and four over-coats that his wardrobe contained that day. On his wrists, white gold cuff-links. 'I won't touch anything else.' After the show, the sartorial trend-setter went to a first-night party in Mayfair. He hit the pillow at 5.30 a.m.

Who knows whether his own presence on stage for the London opening might have softened the critics; instead, they gave *Maggie May* the kind of hammering that could deafen a shipbuilder. Despite praise for the sets, the dancing, the production, the dialogue and the acting, *The Times* concluded:

> Mr Bart's ultimate destination is, of course, a sort of folk opera with its music created from the eclectic anthology of styles in which he works. In the amount of music he has composed for *Maggie May*, he is probably nearer to his aim than in any earlier show. One or two of his tunes have an exciting rhythmic vigour, but those which stay in the mind are those he has taken from tradition; melodically, the others have little to give either to their lyrics or to the audience.

The *Express*, too, had nothing but praise for 'the best acted musical for many a day', as it did for the sets and production, but: 'Not every-thing is so perfect. The chief fault of the show is length, and there are some sagging sections in the second half when Alun Owen's slight story of union trouble on the docks is left to meander in a somewhat meaningless circle, and the songs begin to feel tiring.'

With a few days to compose its thoughts and reactions, the *Sunday Telegraph* began with an echo of Bart's own sentiments about the sclerotic nature of West End producers and managements:

> It is ironic that Mr Peter Cadbury is selling tickets for *Maggie May* at the Adelphi. For, on the surface anyway, this Alun Owen–Lionel Bart musical could be branded as one of those 'dirty plays' which he and Mr Emile Littler believe are degrading our bright, clean, innocent West End stage...The British North, through the novels of John Braine and Alan Sillitoe, the plays of Alun Owen and Shelagh Delaney, with some additional help from the Beatles, has become for Southern audiences a Grimm's folktale country where everyone drinks deep, loves hard, fights long and swears loud on an industrial battlefield.

Maggie May, the reviewer concludes, is better than *Blitz!* 'But both book and music appear intermittent and unintegrated, given to odd pauses and repetitions. And musically Mr Bart is often torn between Brecht and the Beatles. He is at his best when he relies for inspiration on that great composer "Traditional" with snatches of sea shanties and folk songs woven into simple, direct, flowing melody.

'I said it was better than *Blitz!* But for those who believe in setting their standards by *Pal Joey*, *Guys and Dolls* and *West Side Story*, better than *Blitz!* is not good enough.'

Did it matter to Bart? Nothing could stop him. Every public utterance was accompanied by his natty new creed: 'Go Bart Go!' Nothing could even momentarily slow him down. In June 1964 the *Sunday Express* published the heart-breaking story of an East End bookmaker's daughter, little 'Teresa O'Brien, fourteen-year-old polio cripple', who had sung for Bart two years earlier. 'And ever since she has looked forward to playing a part written for her in his new musical. But this weekend Teresa's parents will try to break the news – there is no part for her after all.' It is tempting to wonder whether, after two years, a bright girl like Teresa might not have suspected as much herself...or indeed, why it took her parents two years to find the right moment to break it to her. Speaking from her council flat at Old Ford Road, Bethnal Green, Mrs Eileen O'Brien explained how Lionel promised to write a special part for her daughter in *Maggie May*. 'We have never heard from him since. I am disgusted. I thought that this part would give Teresa a real lift and make up for her handicap. It would not have been so bad if we had been told definitely that it was off. But we never heard anything.'

Teresa had been taken to see Bart at the New Theatre by Mrs Kathleen O'Connor, who was then Mayor of Stepney and had heard her sing at a local concert. Georgia Brown also showed an interest, taking her for an audition with a teacher at the Wigmore Hall, ostensibly for lessons prior to joining the cast. Teresa herself takes up the story: 'Mr Bart was very nice to me at the theatre. After I sang, he came up to me on the stage and went down on his knees, took my hands and said, "Darling, you were marvellous." He said he would write this special part for me in *Maggie May*. I thought it was wonderful. Everyone was so pleased about it. I really thought he meant it. I'm still hoping. But whatever happens, I still want to be a singer.'

Those *Sunday Express* readers whose eyes had not by now filled with tears of sympathy, could read Lionel's response a little further down the column. 'It is not true that I have forgotten Teresa. I think about her all the time. I liked her very much and I thought she had a lovely voice. I did say I would try to put her in *Maggie May*. But at that time it was all in the remote distance, and I did not make a definite promise. As things have worked out, the only juvenile part will be for a little girl of ten with a Liverpool accent. If Teresa thinks I have let her down, I will write her a note and explain what has happened. I am sorry everyone thought I had definitely promised a part for her. But I am always writing new shows. Perhaps one day there will be a part for Teresa.'

Had Lionel now become too busy to remember such details? Because of the way Lionel's hats often sat perched on the top of his head, there was a joke going round his friends that he always bought them too small. The joke going round his enemies was that his head wouldn't stop growing out of them. He was now at the head of a showbusiness empire worth over £1 million. He had a male secretary: 'There's a status symbol for you,' claimed the *Daily Mirror*. He had a string of loosely run companies, each witness to the diversity of his assets:

– *The Apollo Music Company* held publishing rights and promoted new talent. It later gave the world 'Concrete and Clay' by Unit Four Plus Two.
– *Oliver Productions Limited* and *Oliver Promotions*[12] handled the show, plus spin-offs and merchandising.
– *Blue Valley Music Company* was another publishing title.
– *Trelion Music* was associated with pianist Russ Conway.
– *Solihull Music* looked after the Applejacks.
– *Moss Music* was formed to publish all the film compositions of the Rolling Stones.
– *Forward Look* was formed with Andrew Oldham, the Stones' manager, with the objective of producing records and discovering young promise. Their first release was 'As Tears Go By' recorded by sixteen-year-old Marianne Faithfull, who was still at convent school.
– *G and B Arts* was a design and print company, founded with John Gorman.
– *Lionel Bart Limited* was a tax benefit.
– *Lionel Bart Films* had two treatments in development: one, with Associated British, was a biopic of Ralph 'Gang Show' Reader's life. The other, starring the Rolling Stones, was to be co-funded by Peter Sellers's Brookfield and by Columbia.

Add to these the income from productions of *Oliver!* around the world: it had been running for two years in New York, and had opened in Sydney, Melbourne, Durban, Johannesburg, Stockholm, Amsterdam and the Sudan, with offers pending from Russia, Czechoslovakia, Hungary, Israel and France. Song royalties poured in from around four million sales of records. One song alone – 'As Long As He Needs Me' – had been recorded by around 300 different singers and groups. Film rights and options on the stage shows were being sold and resold as they expired unmade. And other films needed him more than he needed them. For their latest James Bond movie, Cubby Broccoli and Harry Saltzman approached Bart to come up with a song which would fit over the Bond theme, but which would work equally well out of context and would not give away the film's plot in its lyric. Bart had one of his most successful songs in 'From Russia With Love', although its original recording was by a relatively unknown Matt Monro, who had been cutting demo acetates along with Vince Hill at thirty shillings apiece, because they both sang as passable impersonations of Frank Sinatra. His other 1964 film credit was considerably less auspicious. Being her usual rebellious self, Joan Littlewood was seemingly prepared to sacrifice everything and everyone to her vision, which was then to make a movie. Perversely, she chose *Sparrers Can't Sing*,[13] and insisted (against the wishes of the backers) that Barbara Windsor should star. Bart wrote a hauntingly beautiful song which she sings over the credits, and which is probably the most memorable aspect of the entire misguided and painfully produced work.

Bart was in demand – unstoppable and unquenchable demand. He had made it, and others demanded to know how. He was a willing guru to the newly born chart industry of hit singles and beat groups. He still kept a foot in the Tommy Steele–Cliff Richard camp. He was at the hub of the theatre world, hanging round the dressing-rooms of his four shows. He was about to make more movies. He was the keystone of London's glitterati. It was to be expected, then, that this scion of the sixties should find himself spinning atop the other swingers. As Bart tells it, he was appointed trustee of the Rolling Stones, since their own manager, Andrew Oldham, had not reached the age of majority, and thus could not sign any legal contracts on their behalf.[14] At any rate, the two were indisputably in business together in the summer of '64, and had teamed up to promote a company for writing songs and handling singers.

Their meeting, in Bart's anecdotage, is picaresque. Lionel was lunching one day in the summer of '62 with Pablo Picasso. Together they strolled along the Croisette in Cannes, looking for a fish restaurant which the painter enjoyed. Their pleasant walk in the sun was then interrupted by 'this young, redheaded guy, and he's English, and he stops me, and he tells me he'd been stranded there...his parents had gone back to England, and he was trying to get the fare together, and would I help him with the equivalent of £5 in francs, which was quite a lot in those days for a kid to be turning on the street. But I gave it to him, and he told me his name was Andrew Loog Oldham. He gave me a card, and on the card it said MANAGER, and I said, "What are you managing?" and he said, "Oh, pop groups and singers," and he was in a band, so I said, "Well, come and see me when you get back to London." And we went off to eat. And while I'm eating, Picasso said, "Regarde ton ami"...and we looked out the window of the restaurant, and watched the boy score off about twelve punters, presumably the same amount of money as he'd had off me. And I thought, I'm not having that, and on the way back he was still there on the job, so I said, "OK, give me back my bloody money, you sod, I've been watching you on the make...but you can still come and see me in London." And I forgot about it...until a couple of months later, he turned up at Apollo Music, and he was still only sixteen or seventeen, and managing the Rolling Stones by now...and I became a sort of role model for him, I suppose. I was wearing black Borsalino hats and black woollen scarves that my housekeeper used to knit, and so consequently he had to have Borsalino hats and black scarves, and we'd go around Soho together and we became buddies. He was into early Tamla Motown and Phil Spector, and because he was too young officially to be their manager, I became a guarantor, and all the Stones' works were serviced through my publishing company. And it was around this time that Mick Jagger and Keith Richards stayed in my empty mews flat. Mick was with Chrissie Shrimpton at the time, and Keith with Anita Pallenberg. I remember at the time leaving a case of KY Jelly behind at the Mews, and Mick telling Chrissie it was hair gel...so she'd go out with her head covered in KY Jelly!'

No matter that Mr Oldham, like his colleague Mr Bart, was incapable of writing a musical note; together, they put their musical thoughts into letters of the tonic sol-fa for later transcription to the stave. At the time Oldham was boastful of their joint ignorance, claiming that 'a knowledge of music is a hindrance. We prefer what I call professional amateurism.' Their first disc together featured the Stones with their seven-teen-year-old friend and the daughter of an Austrian baroness, Marianne Faithfull. On the flipside? Bart's new 'arrangement' (though estrangement may have been more apt) of 'Greensleeves'. The Stones were chasing the Beatles for world supergroup status that year thanks to 'Not Fade Away', and had just released 'It's All Over Now' on Decca. And yet in the American charts, although the Beatles were logging number ones with every record they cut (it was the year of the title track from *A Hard Day's Night*), second place overall in the Top Twenty was held for weeks by Louis Armstrong, with Dave Clark in third place.

Andrew Loog Oldham (he had adopted both his parents' surnames at the time) is the illegitimate war-child of a wealthy English mother and a Dutch-American bomber pilot who was killed before his son's birth. Oldham is increasingly billed alongside Brian Epstein as one of the first tycoons of pop, with an influence already compared to that other music Svengali of the time, Phil Spector. In 1964 he was nineteen, a sharp dresser who looked not unlike Andy Warhol, forever photographed alongside Mick Jagger or Keith Richards in matching large collars or reefer jackets and yachting caps. As a teenager hanging around the Soho coffee bars, he had already decided that he wanted to be 'where the car-pets are thick and the tea-cups are thin'. He drifted from a job as Mary Quant's runner to selling illegal drinks in nightclubs. He cut a few dud singles under aliases such as Sandy Beach or Chancery Lane. He was publicist for Mark Wynter, Little Richard and the Beatles before becoming manager and producer of the Stones in April 1963. With Bart he hatched a barely credible plan to devise two ballets. This is how Bart described the enterprise that seems never to have matured: 'It's still very much in the discussion stage. I have never been involved in ballet before, apart from watching it. Andrew is devising two ballets. I shall be writing the music for one and helping with the other. We are thinking of a com-pletely new form of presentation involving electronics and stereophonic sound. We want to get Paddy Stone to do the choreography and Sean Kenny to design the sets. My mind is already beginning to tick over on the ideas, but it will take at least two months before we can really get down to it.'

A propensity for exaggeration was something the two men shared, then as now. Oldham had established his business (he was also managing Herman's Hermits among others) in lavish offices overlooking Regent's Park. He had donated to himself all the necessary trappings and affectations of success in the music industry: a stately home in Kent, an ankle-length leather coat and six cars, including the Roller with chauffeur, record-player, telephone and bar. But by 1967 his brightest star had waned. His control over the Stones was passed to another manager, Allen Klein, and Bart sensed that some heat might be turned on him over the early 'contracts'. 'People would have killed for those contracts. But there was a lot of suing going on involving some Mafia contacts and ABCo, which I later discovered was supposed to stand for A Better Kind of Company, and all I wanted was a quiet life, so I tore the contracts up. I wasn't a business person. I wasn't then, and I still ain't.' If he had been, he might have asked for a percentage of 'As Tears Go By' which he claims to have 'messed about on a bit with the lyric', as he also thinks he did with 'Satisfaction (I Can't Get No)'. But then, it was all just a family thing: Mick helped Bart write 'Carrying On', the opening Act Two song of *Maggie May* (Bart now thinks it sounds like the jazz classic 'Green Onions'), just as Bart made Paul McCartney rethink the lyric of 'Eleanor Rigby'. 'Paul had come round to ask me for my approval for something he'd written while we were walking my two alsatians, Simon and Garfunkel, around the cemetery on Wimbledon Common. And while we were there, we'd seen a family headstone for Ann and Eleanor Bygraves. But when he sat down at my clavichord and sang it, I wasn't too happy...because I wasn't too happy about Max Bygraves at the time...and made him change it to Rigby.'

Oldham went on briefly to run a record label at the end of the sixties with Tony Calder, which provided the world with 'Hang on Sloopy', but then disappeared from view, and only resurfaced in the mid-1990s, after almost two decades in Bogotá, with seemingly few regrets: 'The pace of my life might have changed, but I never really came down from the sixties. The party never really stopped.' Today he shows selective recall of the days of wine and poses, with outrageous tales of taking acid with a member of the royal family or smoking dope with Picasso.

Like the sixties themselves, Lionel showed no sign of easing up on life. During the course of one week he composed 'Too Young for Sad Memories', 'Stiletto Baby' and 'Two Wrongs Don't Make a Right' – all doubtless as memorable as last year's Eurovision entry, but all of them bright sparks flying out of this powerhouse of pop. Did he care about the duodenal ulcer or the dangers of diluting his talent? Of course he did, and yet: 'Sure I'm burning the candle at the ends and in the middle. But maybe at the back of my mind I'm remembering the broken-down gaff we all lived in in Whitechapel when we were pretty poor and when my Dad often had no wages at the end of the week.' And so, the next project was always in sight – or, in this case, in his sights. Bart announced that he had teamed up with Harvey Orkin, theatrical agent and a regular on BBC Television's *Not So Much a Programme...* to write a new jazz musical – based on the legend of Robin Hood. 'It is going to be a naughty show. A very naughty show. Robin is a con-man, Maid Marian is a kookie nymph, and Little John an abject coward. You might describe it as a satirical girlie show that is definitely not for the family trade.'

Remarkably (or possibly not, in view of its Ealing comedy and *Carry On* associations) the entire project had been commissioned by United Artists and Brookfield Productions, a new independent company headed by Peter Sellers and John Bryan.[15] Brookfield was to co-produce the film version for United Artists to release after the stage show had run its course, 'on a lavish scale as the most ambitious of the several projects Brookfield will make for United Artists'. Indeed, George Ornstein, UK head of UA, was publicly declaring that Bart alone stood to make over a million out of the deal.

Without a shadow of embarrassment, Bart declared that the new show would be called *Twang!!* 'with two exclamation marks. On the posters we shall have an arrow quivering in a tree. The show will be sub-titled *The Misadventures of Robin Hood.*' The show was to prove the greatest misadventure of Lionel Bart.

CHAPTER SIX

REVIEWING THE SITUATION

ROBIN HOOD musical in difficulties,
urgently requires kind theatre-loving
financial genius to advise on honorary
basis. No investment required.

W hen this notice appeared in the Personal Column of *The Times* in September 1965, suspicions were immediately aroused that it was yet another setback in the much-bruited troubles plaguing Lionel Bart's *Twang!!* Not so – though Bart might have benefited from some of the replies.

The advertiser was Julian Melgrave, a thirty-year-old writer and managing director of a sales organization in South Africa, who was to make an unexpected appearance the morning after the fateful *Twang!!* disgraced the London stage. Melgrave had written his version ten years prior to Lionel's – five years, in fact, before *Oliver!* The show, called *Hood's Guerilla*, had been reworked some half-dozen times and, by a further curious twist, had been sent in 1961 to Marcus Dods, who had been musical director of *Maggie May*, *Blitz!* and *Oliver!* Dods had turned down the musical, claiming he was 'not particularly impressed' with the music. It was only when reading about Bart's version that Mr Melgrave decided to leave his post in South Africa, and fly to Britain in search of advice on how best to spend the budget he had available for putting on the musical. His advertisement brought several replies, but only a terse

'Nothing to do with us' from the offices of Lionel Bart. Its fate can never have been as costly to its creator as that of *Twang!!* was to be.

Bart and his collaborator Harvey Orkin[1] saw Robin as a medieval wide-boy who became a hero despite himself. Dangerously, Lionel confessed that he found con-men 'very colourful', though he was, to be fair, referring to their ability to be chameleon-like, which made them theatrically rich. 'What we are doing is to satirize the Crusades, the attitude of the Church and, above all, human gullibility which can turn an outlawed man into some kind of heroic saint.' But perhaps the overall tone of the show is best summed up by two early numbers Bart had composed (neither of which appears to have made it to the final version). 'Locksmith for the Lady' was to be sung by a line of pretty, leggy ladies encased in chastity belts by their husbands, who have naughtily gone off to the Crusades and left them behind to go rusty. In essence, the song is their lament, expressing their determination to secure the services of a friendly locksmith (or a stupid one) who will liberate them from this stifling predicament. This amusing ditty is followed by another maidens' chorus, in which the newly emancipated and unshackled wives chirrup about their immediate availability. The title? 'Thou Hath It Made'.

Originally slated to open in Birmingham for ten performances at the start of a pre-London tour, the production was suddenly rescheduled for the Palace Theatre, Manchester, on 3 November 1965, because 'additional time has been found necessary for preparation'. The citizens of Birmingham did not take to the streets. The London opening date was unchanged: the Shaftesbury on 8 December. It was but one of the minor detours on the show's road to ruin. With a fortnight to go before the first night, Bart wrote to the production associates to ask for a change of billing. Perhaps scenting disaster, he wanted the credits to read 'Joan Littlewood's *Twang!!* with music and song-words by Lionel Bart'. The disclaimer was disallowed. It went on – and shortly thereafter came off – as 'Joan Littlewood's production of Lionel Bart's *Twang!!*'

Throughout the London rehearsals that October the press had been gorging itself on black gossip about the rows and feuds between Bart and his director, about the tears and the tantrums of overwrought and overworked talents, about the walk-outs and the vendettas. Bored with

Stratford, Joan wanted to build her utopian Fun Palace – a kind of upmarket, cultural theme park for experimentation and amusement. To do this, she needed money. Very large amounts of money. According to Lionel, 'Joan loved to screw with the Establishment and turn the tables...that was her game. And here we had the Establishment embracing us and *giving* us money.' Presumably, on the strength of Lionel and Joan's joint reputation. But neither reputation needed any additional polish; the driving-force had gone.

Bart's memory of the sorry saga is shot through with bitterness. 'We were often rehearsing in the gardens at my house in Seymour Walk...actors everywhere, dancers limbering up...and Joan constantly wanting to change things. "Can't have it too cosy," she said. "Let's get a bit of danger in it." Oliver Messel had produced some high camp designs based on medieval books of hours, which were exquisite, but the undergarments of the dancers were made of fabric so rich and so heavy, Joan told them to put them on the ground and jump on them to soften them up. The leaves on the trees in Sherwood Forest were made of the most expensive green velvet. Paddy Stone[2] would set movement to a song, and the next day Joan would come in and say, "Lovely, but we can't use it, because we're not doing that number." She left. I left. Script-doctors came in. Before we even opened we were a household name – bad news. There was enormous conflict.'

Barbara Windsor has two theories that go some way to explaining the breakdown of the partnership and of the show. 'She did exactly what she did with *Fings*. She thought she was with a dozen actors and a few old props, saying "Invent!" But you cannot do a big musical like that. It's got to be organized. Instead, she tore up the script, and told the showgirls in the chorus-line just to do their own thing! It *should* have been wonderful, but we knew from the day we went in that *we'd* all changed. When we'd all got together before, when we'd done *Fings*, we just wandered on stage and did it. You can't do that in a West End musical, and what's more, we were famous now.' Searching eyes, in other words, were upon them all.

Rising above the mayhem (for the moment) was the show's man in tights James Booth (veteran of con-man roles), who had already worked with Miss Littlewood and Bart on *Fings*, and who had turned down two big-buck Hollywood pictures to play Robin – an odd piece of casting, perhaps, revealed when one London critic wrote that he could not 'even Rex Harrison his way out of the songs'. Booth defended the two antagonists as 'creative egos' who were simply wearing their temperaments on the outside. Yet by the end of November, and with the London opening postponed by two weeks, Mr Booth became doleful, and declared that if his part were not improved he would rather withdraw from the show, confessing that parts had not been properly rehearsed and Act Two had not been fully rewritten. Not that rewriting wasn't an hourly occurrence: Ronnie Corbett (playing Will Scarlett) is fond of telling a story about the rehearsal during which he had briefly to excuse himself for a call of nature. On his return, he asked why no one had given him his next cue, only to be told that his line had been cut. Outraged, he appealed to Miss Littlewood: 'Don't ever let me go for a shit, or you'll cut out my entire part!'

Joan Littlewood, of course, did not come without her legends trailing before her: she was once described as having directed Brendan Behan's Irish Republican play *The Hostage* with the aid of a crate of Guinness and a horsewhip. But perhaps her heyday had waned, as Bart's was now waning. The peak of her achievement had been in the mid-1950s with her Theatre Workshop repertory productions, though after a period away from her troupe in the early sixties, she had had a triumphant return in the spring of 1963 with *Oh! What a Lovely War*, which had a year's run at the Wyndham's until June 1964. She was undoubtedly convinced of her own rightness in any matters theatrical, and is reputed to have been reluctant to accept anything which did not fit in with her concept of a production, rarely agreeing to changes even under pressure. She and Bart were not to co-exist in disharmony for long. The day before press night, Joan Littlewood quit the company for good.

On the very night *Twang!!* opened in Manchester, those two exclamation marks were being replaced by a question mark. The reputation of the golden boy of musicals was on the line. After eight years of fabulous success that had brought him close on £2 million, he was staring his first public failure in the face. *Twang!!* was about to be derided by critics and audiences alike. Financial backers – the American film company United Artists and Britain's Brookfield Films – were getting very cold feet about the London transfer, increasingly keen not to throw good money after bad on an over-ambitious, under-prepared production that had already run up bills of £85,000, with little to show for it. After three days of discussions in Manchester with Bart, with script-writer Harvey Orkin and with others in the creative team, impresario Bernard Delfont bowed out as producer, saying only: 'It's much too complicated to go into.' He had, though, no objection to the planned transfer to his London venue, to which Bart responded: 'Frankly, Bernard is the odd man out. This is not a personal thing between him and me. The whole team up here think *Twang!!* is a good show. We are doing wonders with it. Bernard is the only one to differ. Bernard had no money in the show anyway. If we give him a hit, he is doing all right.'

This was somewhat disingenuous of Lionel, who had taken to travelling by chauffeured Cadillac and wearing a flat cap in the North. Only hours before, he was lamenting, 'This is the worst crisis I have ever had in my life.' On 24 November 1965 the curtain failed to go up because Barbara Windsor was suffering from laryngitis and had no understudy. The curtain remained down until the delayed London opening on Monday 20 December, which gave Bart three weeks of day-and-night rewriting and reshaping. It could never be enough.

During the sixties Bernard Delfont put on a dozen musicals in the West End, and twice as many straight plays. His judgment had brought him the satisfaction of launching the partnership of Anthony Newley and Leslie Bricusse (a team whose early success, like Bart's, was never sustained), as well as the career of Michael Crawford. Moreover, the Delfont organization had seen *Maggie May* through a financially shaky year-long run at the Adelphi. It was wayward of Bart not to heed the impresario's early warnings. Delfont saw the problem with *Twang!!* as one of structure: it lacked, in his view, any semblance of one. 'From the very beginning it looked a mess. I put great faith in Joan Littlewood, who proved by the unlikely success of *Fings* that she had the capacity to pull together strands to make an original and satisfying whole. But Lionel was no longer the theatrical novice sensitive to Joan Littlewood's obsession with doing things her way. He had ideas of his own, and when they clashed with those of the director, he fought his corner. The rows were long and furious, culminating on the day before the Manchester opening with Joan Littlewood walking off the show and out of our lives. A newspaper quoted me as saying that I was not a happy man.

'I toyed with the idea of bringing in a script doctor. Burt Shevelove, author of *A Funny Thing Happened on the Way to the Forum*, came to mind. The two shows had in common an anarchic sense of humour which can so easily become self-indulgent. Shevelove might have imposed the discipline of an experienced outsider but he needed more than twenty-four hours to work the magic. Meanwhile, we did a hatchet job on forty minutes of the three-hour show, and hoped for the best.

'It was no good. At one point in the show Barbara Windsor had to say, "I don't know what's going on here." As one, the audience responded "Neither do we." I got the message. I told Lionel and his writer Harvey Orkin that I wanted out, expecting them to follow suit by putting up the white flag. Not a bit of it. After a huddled negotiation they decided to go on without me. Would I still let them have the Shaftesbury Theatre in London? I could hardly say no, though it occurred to me that it wasn't much of a favour. I gave the London run a week at most. It exceeded my expectations by a few days with audiences who presumably had not read the appalling notices. The débâcle was a punishing blow to Lionel's career.'

Even before the Manchester opening, the newspapers had scented blood – Bart's blood – and they were thirsty for it. Like Tamburlaine, he had (not only in their eyes) overreached himself. He was overdue for a fall, and although he knew it, he was putting it off in the most fatally costly way imaginable. Despite all advice from Noël never to put money into one's own shows, Bart told the backers that if anyone got cold feet, *he* would come in with his own resources ('That was the least I could do'). It could not have been a more disastrous decision: even in the best of all possible worlds, the gardener is too deeply and lovingly attached to his creation to be able to see it with the eyes of one who identifies the need for pruning, mowing, digging and retrenching. Bart was to become his own master and, in taking overall control, he allowed him-

LEFT Although it is commonly believed that Lionel's theatrical education began at Joan Littlewood's Theatre Workshop, he was already closely involved with the agit-prop Unity Theatre by 1952, writing several songs for the revue *Turn It Up*, as well as appearing as one of the Ugly Sisters in *Cinderella*. (1,2)

ABOVE In a matter of months, the washboard player of Tommy Steele's Cavemen had graduated from Beatnik to West End and waistcoats, with movies like *Tommy the Toreador* and transfers of his first two musicals *Fings Ain't Wot They Used t'Be* and *Lock Up Your Daughters*. (3)

ABOVE Leaving behind the family name and the family home in Stamford Hill, Lionel Begleiter adopted the name of a London hospital and adapted easily to the luxuries of South Kensington. Despite appearances, he is still unable to read notes on a stave. (4)

Legend has it that this advertisement (INSET) on the back page of the *Sunday Pictorial* in 1959 gave Bart the inspiration to write 'Living Doll'. Although Cliff Richard originally recorded the song for the film *Serious Charge* (ABOVE) he was unhappy with the treatment and re-released it as the single that went to number one. Almost thirty years later it did so again, thanks to The Young Ones. (5, 6)

LEFT Not one to read Dickens for inspiration, Bart took the idea for a musical about Oliver Twist from the image of a chocolate-bar hero of his childhood asking for 'More'. (7)

RIGHT Though eventually rewarded with success, neither Ron Moody nor Georgia Brown was first choice as Fagin and Nancy. In this scene from the original production of 1960, Bill Sikes is played by Danny Sewell. Barry Humphries was also in the cast. (8)

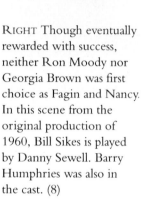

BELOW Triumphant after seeing *Oliver!* become the longest-running musical in British theatre history, Bart forgets the tribulations of *Twang!!* for a few hours to throw a Christmas party in 1965 for cast members and 100 children from Barnardo's homes. (9)

ABOVE Inspiration can strike, even in snakeskin boots and a Bentley. Bart was inseparable from a tape-recorder, his only way of recalling a song. (10)

RIGHT The Brits on Broadway – Jonathan Miller, Anna Quayle, Peter Cook, Alan Bennett, Vivien Leigh and Dudley Moore join Bart to collect their Tony Awards on 29 April 1963. (11)

ABOVE Alma Cogan had inexplicably proposed marriage to Lionel on *This Is Your Life*. From being the sun around which many lesser stars revolved in the late fifties and early sixties, she herself quickly burned out, and died in 1966. They are seen here arriving as a couple at the first night of *Maggie May* on 22 September 1964 at the Adelphi. (12)

BELOW One of the few obsessions Bart quickly grew out of was the need to own several vehicles, particularly expensive marques: Facel Vega, Morgan, Bentley, Mercedes, Riley and this Karmann Ghia, outside the flat in Reece Mews, where Francis Bacon was Bart's next-door neighbour. (13)

Despite having conquered the West End with *Fings*, in 1965 Joan Littlewood (ABOVE) was unable to rescue *Twang!!* and is partly accused of shooting it into oblivion, along with Lionel's bank account. BELOW Barbara Windsor was a nymphomaniac princess, James Booth a rakish Robin Hood in what has become a byword for theatrical fiasco. *The Times* pondered: 'There is often something mystifying in the way that musicals swallow up prodigious investments of money and yield nothing in return.' The *Daily Express* was less reserved in its judgement, denouncing the disaster as 'a shambling ragbag of mediocre ideas badly executed'. (14, 15, 16)

ABOVE Drawing on Lionel's own childhood memories of his mother and aunts making ends meet during the war, *Blitz!* (1962) had a sentimentality that made some critics wince. Once again, Sean Kenny's sets became the most impressive creation on stage. (17)

RIGHT Sartorially suspect, Bart arrives at court on 17 February 1971 in a chauffeur-driven Daimler, having opted for an unusually sober brown tweed and dark kipper tie. The charge was for possession of eight grams of cannabis resin. (18, 19)

ABOVE By his own admission more than two stones overweight, Bart today resents being wheeled out to receive tributes. With Adam Faith, he returns to the scene of his early musical discoveries to unveil the plaque marking the birth of rock 'n' roll at the 2 I's coffee bar in Soho. (20)

BELOW 'I have looked over the edge more than most.' (21)

self to do everything – and nothing. Without a strong producer to rein him in, he became reckless. There is a vintage showbusiness story, often told on occasions such as these, concerning the long-dead musical *My Dear Public*. It was produced by Irving Caesar, co-written by Irving Caesar, had lyrics by Irving Caesar and was co-composed by Irving Caesar. The notices killed the show. On the morning after the first night, Caesar called Oscar Hammerstein. 'OK,' he admitted, 'the critics didn't like it. The public didn't like it. But why pick on me?'

As Bart saw it, the *Twang!!* problem was simply financial: he argued that if the show were allowed a dignified burial in Manchester, the backers would lose £100,000. If, as he hoped, the show transferred to London and perished instantly, the loss would be £130,000. He was eager to risk that £30,000 to prove a point – to prove that a worthless satire on Sherwood green was another Bart masterpiece. His past and his future were both in the balance, yet he was holding the scales and tampering with the weights. As he paced his hotel room in Manchester in the middle of the bloody battle being waged around him, the man who would be Napoleon was puffed up with fighting talk: 'I am determined never to give up. I have never had to deal with a scene like this before, but I'm meeting it as a challenge. Right from the start I have wanted to go to London, and fail if necessary. That first night here in Manchester, when it was clear what was happening, I couldn't wait for the show to end so I could start work on it. The show was my idea, and I have written the songs for it, but during rehearsals it moved so far away from the original conception that it just wasn't my show. Yet I had to take the blame for it. I recommended Joan Littlewood, whom I idolized, to produce it. But as things worked out, my contribution to the original show was little.

'What angered and bewildered the critics and the audience was that the scenes had no relation to the songs. Now, for the past two weeks, we have been giving the show clarity and logicality. But it's not been easy. From the word go we had defeatism in high places. I've had to be a diplomat. Now we've virtually rewritten the play. I've written seven new songs. But the big trouble has been that the actors are so tired. They have had to learn new lines and new songs while going on each night and performing. They've been bloody marvellous in the teeth of rumour promulgated by all kinds of people. We've been having meetings until the small hours of the morning, and I've been working into the smaller hours. In the fortnight, I've had an average of four hours' sleep a night. The last two nights I haven't got to bed at all.

'I wrote a new song for Bernard Bresslaw[3] one night and he performed it the next. He had the lyrics written on scenery trees and even on the floor. James Booth has had his lines scribbled all over his clothes and arms... But this kind of crisis isn't new. My main feeling about this show was one of frustration. I knew that one day, sooner or later, I would have a flop. What has annoyed me with *Twang!!* is that I was taking the responsibility for something that was no longer mine. If, when I have got the show to my standards, it is still a flop, then I'll be able to accept it more readily. It's a terrible thing to be hung for a crime you haven't committed. But this business has done one thing for me. I have found some real friends. The rumours have been terrible. I've had to get on the blower all the time to me mum and dad in London and tell them the true facts – because, you know, their whole life revolves around me.

'The reaction of my friends fell into three categories. There were the people who suddenly crossed me off their list. Then there were the people who couldn't wait to phone me and say with a certain amount of pleasure, "We hear you've got a flop." And thirdly, there were the people who turned out to be true friends. I've had some letters from people I haven't seen for eight years. You know, this has been a turning point in my life. I have found that if you have a flop – and I think you must accept that everyone has a right to a flop – I know for certain that I have friends.' Later that same day, in the deserted bar of a vast theatre only one-third full, a large brandy and Coke helped him recover some of his bravura. 'I have to face the question: Is this my first flop? All I want now is the chance to let the public answer the question. I don't want to appear over-confident at this stage, but I think we can do it. That is, if I stay on my feet.'

Perhaps the cruellest irony in all this is that three days later, on Saturday 20 November 1965, Nicolette Roeg and Aubrey Woods, cast members of *Oliver!*, were serving champagne to the audience at the

New Theatre in London's St Martin's Lane, where the show had been running since opening night for 2,284 performances, making it the longest-running musical in British theatre history. It topped by one the 2,283 performances of *Salad Days*, leaving *My Fair Lady* in third place with 2,282.[4] But Lionel was in no mood for celebration.

The London transfer *was* going ahead, with the revised opening date of 20 December, fulfilling Lionel's self-made prophecy that *Twang!!* would open in the capital before Christmas. It was now being presented by Brookfield Productions alone, with a little help to come from Bart's own pocket – 'and I wouldn't do that unless there was some point, would I?' Yet the point was becoming increasingly lost in Bart's crazedly determined machinations. Bernard Delfont and his partner Arthur Lewis had honourably kept the Shaftesbury Theatre (which was under their joint control) available for the transfer, in spite of their repeated advice that it was an unwise move. With a few hours' breathing space, Bart left some of his worries behind in Manchester and returned to town to hold a party for *Oliver!* Next, he hosted a street party for a hundred children from homes around the capital. Led by the band of the Irish Guards and a float carrying children from the cast, the Dr Barnardo's orphans marched from the Old Curiosity Shop near Kingsway, along the Strand to the New Theatre where the musical was playing. Once there, they were greeted by the Mayor of Westminster, Alderman Sir Charles Norton, and by Lionel himself. On stage were tables covered with food, and for the next two hours nobody needed to ask for More! Then came one of the peculiar requests which were becoming familiar to the prolific composer. Major C. H. 'Jiggs' Jaegar, senior director of music for the Brigade of Guards, invited Lionel to write a regimental march entitled 'Marching Up the Mall'. 'I've always been a fan of Mr Bart,' he explained. And, before returning to the anxieties of rewrites on Act Two, Bart replied: 'I'm delighted, flattered. *Twang!!* permitting, I'll knock off a march this week. I've had at least one in all my shows, but I've never written one specifically for an Army band before. This is a great honour.'

And the festivities went on... A fortnight before Christmas Bart put his current woes behind him for an evening by joining 600 other guests on the stage of the New Theatre at a party hosted by Donald Albery. James Booth also forgot about *Twang!!* and his arguments with Bart for a few hours to cheer Lionel as, with Dame Margot Fonteyn, he cut a six-foot-square birthday cake decorated to look like the poster for *Oliver!* With pressure mounting, Bart was limiting his rabble-rousing in the hope of stalling the newspapers' Cassandra pronouncements. In the two weeks leading up to *Twang!!*'s West End première, he spoke only to the *Sunday Times*. Dressed improbably for the accompanying photograph in his khaki mohair outfit, with epaulettes, a heavy army belt and oversize cowboy boots, he made what sounded like a last-minute call for a truce.

'I started in this business for fame, money, artistic satisfaction and group communication, in that order. Now artistic satisfaction is what I want most. I've got the fame and the money, but I've found they've got out of control. I also have this lunatic desire to stimulate people and be liked for it. I've got a company of fifty people with the same desire. I've got to get it right for them. After all, they've got to go out there on the stage and expose themselves. If you are presenting something to the public, you are up for grabs, whether you are Joe Doakes or Richard Rodgers. One of the showbiz greats rang me up from America the other day and said, "Bart, you must be out of your head, talking publicly about all the comings and goings and trials and tribulations." When he does a show, all he says is "What problems?" Well, it's now been completely rewritten since Manchester and in eight days it's judgment day. It's just an entertainment, which I hope will please people. It's not Vietnam or Rhodesia, though some people think it's been the Battle of Britain. Yeh, perhaps it is like a battle. So why do you think I've got my battledress on?'

One of the new foot soldiers was, following Bernard Delfont's suggestion, Burt Shevelove as replacement director, who was reported to be collecting jokes from Denis Norden and, via what were in those days phenomenally expensive transatlantic telephone calls, from Jack Benny and Bob Hope's massive archives. Even those big guns failed to knock the audience into submission. Everything was tried: two songs were cut out in the hours before the curtain went up, and a sudden decision appears to have been taken to camp everything up – even to add some gleeful transvestism, leading one reviewer to lament: 'It is a re-working of the Robin Hood legend, but so lacking in heroics that there is hardly a man on stage who does not affect the prance of a male model, anxious only to get back home and put his hair in curlers.' Denis Norden recalls being a kind of sounding-board in the later stages of rehearsal: 'It was desperation stakes after Manchester, and it was a question of making decisions very quickly, not about what should be done, but what was the better alternative of desperate measures.' And Harvey Orkin appears to have sensed doom from early on: 'I knew we were in trouble when I started working with Joan. I knew we were in trouble when there were too many points of view which resulted in no point of view at all.' And this was one of the major complaints: to satirize a moment in history or a legendary character, one needs to establish very quickly the exact butt of that satire. Here it was all too vague, unfocused, inconsequential.

The plot of *Twang!!*, in as much as anything resembling one could be isolated from the catastrophe, concerns the efforts of Robin Hood and his Merrie Men to break into Nottingham Castle in a variety of preposterous disguises, in order to prevent a marriage between the nymphomaniac court tart Delphina (Barbara Windsor, whose un-regal accent is blamed on having had a Cockney wet nurse) and the hairy Scots laird Roger the Ugly (Philip Newman looking like a sheepdog), arranged for the purpose of securing the loan of Scottish troops for bad Prince John (Maxwell Shaw, dressed like a panto principal boy). Its mock-folkloric first night has become part of theatre folklore for distinctly unwanted reasons. Even today Barbara Windsor (who had never known a flop until that moment) reminds herself of its awfulness. 'Whenever I'm in a show that's not doing so well, I think of *Twang!!* because if one can survive that, one can survive anything...'

The first-night audience was certainly more carefully orchestrated than the cast. Sean Connery was filmed arriving, Millicent Martin posed for a few flashbulbs, Bernard Levin ducked in with sharpened pen, David Frost beamed for the cameras...and Lionel grinned a little sheepishly as he entered the foyer alone. 'That opening night was just bizarre, a fiasco. James Booth came on for his second-act number in the baggiest tights you've ever seen. The house-lights were going up and down every ten minutes. The exit doors were wide open. And ten minutes before the end, a claque came in to barrack and boo. It could have been a vendetta... They could have been friends of Joan... I'll never know.' From the stage the picture was hardly different, according to Barbara Windsor. 'The musical director collapsed on the first night, and we had to get a dep in. The second half of the show hadn't been scored, so what had been an orchestra in the first half sounded like a trio in the second half. There were rows and fights backstage. At the end James Booth didn't want to go on stage for a curtain-call, although I don't actually remember anybody booing, I do recall that as we went on and sang the closing medley, people just walked out and left us with an empty theatre.'

As the curtain fell there was a moment's hesitation before the audience howled its chorus of disapproval. From the gallery came clear signs of relief as someone sighed: 'Thank God that's over.' Amid all the booing and jeering from the first-nighters, a lone voice from the circle was heard shouting back at them: 'If you don't like it, get out. They are artistes down there, doing their best. Give them a chance.' Noble sentiments, nobly expressed, and no doubt nobly felt, coming, as they did, from that protector of Barbara Windsor's honour (and her former employer) – Danny La Rue. Nevertheless, there were a few other supporters in the audience, and enough applause to support five curtain calls – though some reports insist it was three, with only a three-minute ovation. And, to this day, Lionel maintains that his creation was merely 'previous. It was just meant to be a camp romp, and I've no doubt someone will do it one day as it should have been done.'

On that day, however, for once the critics honked in unison at the pseudo-pantomime which was pre-empting the more traditional and recognizable Christmas favourite by five goodwill-free days. Recalling the painful gestation in Manchester, Arthur Thirkell told his *Daily Mirror* readers: 'A load of old rubbish was thrown out after the Northern fiasco. And it has been replaced with a lot of brand new rubbish. The only memorable song up to the interval was the National Anthem.' Though satisfied with Oliver Messel's designs (damned elsewhere as 'dull scenery'), the drama critic of *The Times* was more scornful of the entertainment itself: 'The show that inhabits these elegant surroundings seems intended as a Cockney *Camelot*. James Booth, as the outlaw, repeats his usual grinning spiv routine...even King Richard, returning from the Crusades, seems to have come no farther than Brick Lane.' In the *Daily Express*, Herbert Kretzmer called Bart's offerings 'the desolate dregs of a once promising notion...the muses seem to have deserted him'. The *Sun* found faint praise for a *Carry On* favourite: 'Miss Windsor does manage to thrust her voice a little farther out than her chest, but no one has found any real use for her vitality.'

Was Bart devastated? Was hell ever frozen over? The fighter fought back at the stage door with the first-night boos (and, doubtless, some booze) still ringing in his ears. First, he denied any catcalls: 'I didn't hear them. I only listened to the success as they cheered.' Next, he had a conspiracy theory to explain the brickbats. 'As for the booing, that was organized. There is no doubt about that. They started even before the curtain was down. There were "plants" in the circle – and when did you last hear anyone in the circle boo? Four men came into their circle seats only after the interval. At the end they really let themselves go!' No doubt Bart saw the hand of Littlewood rallying some of her Stratford mates. Or were they, as his press officer Brian Sommerville explained, 'a couple of Scotsmen in the gallery enjoying themselves'? Above all, Bart seemed relieved that he had made it back to the West End. Still exhausted from the late nights and early mornings, he kept up the quotable patter for the small huddle of reporters urging him to accept defeat.

'I remember the opening night of *Oliver!* – I was desperately unhappy then. But it's in its sixth year now. I think we've got a very good commercial show on our hands. People liked it. There were 200 laughs – 150 of them solid laughs – which makes it about my funniest yet. I can also say that I heard every note and every word of the lyrics. I didn't write it for the critics. I wrote it for Joe Public – and he's going to rave over it. All we have to do now is speed it up a little and get the lines better, and we can run for at least one to two years. This show is a hit!'

And the very next day, this show had a writ. Issued by Julian Melgrave, the South African businessman now living in Knightsbridge and still touting round his own version of the Sherwood saga, it alleged breach of copyright by Lionel Bart in respect of a song in *Twang!!*

entitled 'I'll Be Hanged'. Bart's solicitor, David Jacobs, insisted the writ would be strongly contested.

Bart appeared oblivious, putting on his they-can't-touch-me act for the showbiz editor of the *Sketch*, who turned up for an interview at the 'Fun Palace', Bart's Chelsea house, the morning after the night before. The strain was beginning to show on Bart's unshaven face, as he lolled on the low leather couch beside a crackling log fire, wearing his canary yellow sweater and black hipsters. He had not been to bed all night, and had spent the first part of the morning closeted with his two publicists, deciding how wise it might be to choose some of the worst reviews and use them as advertisements. One by one, he denied the critics' worst judgments, promising that *Twang!!* would still be around in a year's time, and issuing offers of work to critics whose careers would be over with the kind of chutzpah that would get anybody else a punch in the mouth. He was candid enough to admit that when he walked into a nightclub for the first-night party and the band struck up 'Hello Dolly' he was 'a bit choked'. But the show would go on: 'It's great. I smell success. Brian Epstein, Paul McCartney, David Frost...they've all rung me this morning raving and enthusiastic about the show.' What these sixties' luminaries did not yet know was the personal cost to Bart of his bravado. Propping up the show financially with his own funds and with those of United Artists was to cost him soul and body: such was his belief in his mauled musical, he signed a ten-year deal with the film distributors. Under the terms of the agreement, United Artists would receive a half-share in the profits of *all* his future music publishing over the next ten years. 'I had to do the deal and bring it to London, just to show the knockers,' was his disarming reasoning.

With more anticipation and far less patience than in the wait for a royal baby, the papers carried daily progress reports on the almost still-born monster. Heedless to the pleas for mercy from his cast, Bart followed the old Broadway axiom that no musical is ever written – it is always rewritten. He never stopped tinkering: putting back the title song (always enunciated as Terrr-wang) sung by the chorus, and another number 'Unseen Hands', performed on the album by Long John Baldry. The columnists couldn't stop their deathbed chants, even in newspapers of record, with headlines like: 'DECISION ON *TWANG!!* THIS WEEK'; '*TWANG!!* IN LAP OF GODS'; and '*TWANG!!* TO END IN THREE WEEKS – BARRING MIRACLES'. The nation was in a *Twang!!* frenzy. Bart was now turning into a folk hero – some kind of go-it-alone showman who would prove to the world he could do it: he could beat the odds, he could defy Lady Luck. Everyone's hopes were riding on his adrenalin-charged ballsiness to see him through. His every pronouncement was like Henry's battle-cry at Agincourt, fuelled even now by his own fear of failure to live up to his father's expectations.

According to the *Guardian*, however, the show's destiny was in the hands of one man, Mr Peter Cadbury, who saw the evidence in the second week of January 1966. Mr Cadbury was head of the Keith Prowse ticket-booking agency, which alone was selling around £2 million worth of tickets a year. His enjoyment of *Twang!!* could ensure its future or seal its demise, since he and his colleagues from the Combined Theatre Libraries' Association, an organization of seven major ticket agencies, would place significant block bookings if they liked a show. If not, they wouldn't touch it, and would recommend their punters not to. Mr Cadbury was swift to deny such suggestions, however, claiming[5] that he had not even had an opportunity to go to the Shaftesbury Theatre, and that he was not prepared to take the blame for the show's death. In fact, although the main ticket libraries had decided not to 'do a guarantee' on the show, they had so far sold in excess of £4,000 worth of seats. He summed up his defence with a pointed attack.

> The public decides whether any show will run or not: it is their support that keeps it going, and there is no power known to theatre managers that can make a bad show a success or a good one a flop...[The critics] have destroyed themselves as responsible advisers by beating their little drums over anything that appeals to their narrow *avant garde* tastes and panning unmercifully all conventional theatre like *The Sound of Music* and many other outstanding successes. The British public does not share the critics' passion for sexual perversions and dreary duologues between actors buried in sand or sitting in dustbins – nor do I!

Such sentiments might give Bart some moral capital, but his financial capital was draining away. At the beginning of the third week of the run (more of a hobble, by now) he was admitting that takings had been below the figure agreed with the theatre owners, and to compensate for this, he signed a personal cheque that Monday morning for nearly £5,000, as he had done for the past three weeks. He finally acknowledged, 'It has cost me a lot of money. I would be prepared to finance it to the end of my own resources to prove that it is good entertainment. But my financial advisers might decide that I have gone far enough. This is the crucial week. If we don't move to a more central part of the West End or the takings do not improve, it will probably have to come off. Support is getting better every week and it is heartening. But word of mouth recommendation is working too slowly to combat the three months of bad, "anti-publicity" we got, and bad reviews. I have been working on the show ever since the London opening, and we think we finally have it just right now. That was not my show. This is. Now it is slick and bright, and people are cheering it. But it's too late – the damage was already done. I would invite all the critics to come back and see it again, but I'm too cross with them all.'

Two days later, on 14 January, notice was given. He called the cast of fifty on stage at the Shaftesbury Theatre after the performance, and told them that *Twang!!* was to close on Saturday 29 January 1966, with total losses of over £80,000. Leading man James Booth, who had threatened to walk out in Manchester, could not disguise his relief, particularly since he was scheduled to start work on a film the following month. 'I've had enough of this,' he sighed. But Barbara Windsor appeared genuinely upset. 'I am very sad. So is everybody who has been connected with it. It is a really good show. We were all expecting it to last, but the critics and papers hammered it to death. Lots of well-known people like Sean Connery came to see us and said it was very good. Lionel's very upset.'

At a press conference in the stalls immediately afterwards, Bart puffed on a cigarette and was evidently not too upset to start gushing again. 'Short of flogging my mother's front-room suite, there was nothing more I could do. But there is one piece of good news. Tonight I had a firm offer from one of two Broadway producers who have been after the show. It is now up to me to decide whether to accept or not. I can't talk very much about it because it is up to me to think it over, and I am not at liberty to say the price I have been offered. I also want time to think whether I physically want to put on another show again. I've got a little tired of writing cheques. Now I want to sit down and write some songs.' The Broadway offer was about as firm as marshmallow.

But was it all the fault of the critics? After all, hadn't they panned *The Sound of Music* and *Charlie Girl* – both of which went on to record-breaking runs? Had the sixties' public simply become too sophisticated for an over-elaborate adult pantomime set in Sherwood Forest? These were the days of the burnt bra, of the first man on the moon, of plays about babies being stoned to death in their prams. Even Tim Rice and Stephen Oliver together were unable to stimulate the theatregoing palate with their medieval mayhem in *Blondel* some eighteen years later: and yet this does not account for the ever-running whimsy that is *Cats*. First, a big musical needs a good idea, not necessarily a big idea. It needs meticulous planning and an omnipotent, single unquestionable authority to govern it. United Artists did not wield that authority, neither did Bernard Delfont. Bart and Joan Littlewood had irreconcilable differences about how to stage the show. Time and money were both seen as the necessary panacea: they never are. They failed to save *Carrie* or *Bernadette* or *Children of Eden* or *Hunting of the Snark* or any number of other expensive and worthy attempts that now give off a decomposing stink we lingeringly relish.

Meanwhile, on the home front, Bart had other critics to deal with. Mr George Warne, the builder who did the conversion work on the Chelsea house, dubbed 'a showplace of London's theatrical set', was suing the millionaire for £713 7s 2d, the overdue balance that had remained unpaid for four months. The total bill for the work, labour and materials had been just over £6,000, of which the majority had been paid on account. A short time later he was being sued by Mr Baudouin Mills for £1,000, which he claimed was due to him as an agreed fee for supervising the interior décor. In the High Court on 6

October 1967 Bart denied the allegation, and the courtroom was awed by the grandiose descriptions of showbusiness taste which, according to Mr Rodney Bax, QC, for Mr Mills, might not be to everyone's taste. The court was to hear of 'a lavatory in the form of a Gothic throne with a stone font...of a bathroom in lilac with lilac lavatory paper holder and ashtray...of mechanical sliding curtains...of the young actor who had made a hash of the job and whose work Mr Mills, a twenty-nine-year-old French-Canadian antique dealer, was engaged to put right.' Also at issue, apparently, was an agreement by Bart to buy from Mills about £5,000 worth of antique furniture, which his company would purchase before selling on to Bart with an additional 10 per cent commission – lower than the normal 25 per cent fee because of the assured market.

Mr Bax, QC, went on to describe an itemized schedule of the decoration of the house, floor by floor and room by room, drawn up at a six-hour meeting in Bart's Reece Mews flat. And yet, alleged counsel, 'Mr Bart was very prone to change his mind.' After the work had been completed, Lionel decided that a separate bathroom and lavatory should be knocked into one. This involved knocking down a partition, which left a strip of wall not covered by wallpaper. Mr Mills ascertained that the paper could not be obtained in under two weeks and only from Paris, so Lionel consigned him to Paris to get the paper that day...or the next... and that Mr Mills did. In the event, six months' work grew imperceptibly to twelve.

The bench had heard nothing so salacious since the Profumo affair four years earlier. The private lives of the rich and famous were on public show once again in the most lurid and voyeuristic detail. Bart was alleging that Mills was bringing the action simply out of 'pique' because he was upset at rumours that Bart was claiming credit for his work, but said that as a 'humanist' he had offered Mills £1,000 for liaison work if he could speed up the decoration and have it completed in six months. They were at loggerheads long before the case came to court, as Bart had wanted the house ready to host the party for the opening night of *Maggie May*. Summing up in the two-day battle, Mr Justice Widgery said: 'When the recollections of the parties are as wide apart as they are in this case, then it is clear that one of them is wrong.' Bart had left the court before the judge gave his decision, and later learned by telephone that he had been ordered to pay not only the £1,000 claimed against him, but a further £1,500 costs. His reaction? 'I'm not at all upset by the court's decision. I will treat the £1,000 as a donation to a charity and leave it at that. I've chosen every item of the decorations in my home – right down to the last detail. That includes the lilac loo. It's in a lilac bathroom attached to a lilac bedroom. It all blends in fairly well and is designed for guests. My own loo is in natural pine.'

The house, with its massive artificial rooftop bird, was becoming Bart's heaviest albatross. Noël Coward had dubbed it 'not so much a house, more an amusement arcade', and Bart was mercilessly teased about it by the press and his friends. He had bought the property, formerly called St Dunstan's Priory, in a cul-de-sac just opposite St Stephen's Hospital on Fulham Road, back in December 1963 for around £55,000 – or around forty-eight days' income. He spent a further £115,000 on decorations and alterations, plus another £20,000–30,000 on antique furniture and fittings. By October 1967 it was back on the market...at just £100,000. Bart was doubtless kicking himself for not having accepted an offer of £200,000 made by Rudolf Nureyev shortly after the trial. But, ever Bart, he was defensive about selling it because he needed the cash, preferring instead to claim: 'I built it for a set of values which I am tired of now. I wanted to show off at the time. I wanted to have something sumptuous that belonged to me. Right now I am not all that keen on owning things. Sometimes you finish up feeling that these things really own you. I want something smaller. I felt I was too accessible to callers. I am looking for a cottage at Henley-on-Thames, beside the river.'

Among the many follies consumed by the baroque palace one, at least, was immediately visible (to the chagrin of his many upmarket neighbours) – the ornamental stork nesting on the chimney. Pale green to match the pastel paintwork, and made of a new material (called, very improbably Glamourock), it took a gang of workmen, using block and tackle and scaffolding, over a week to erect, complete with nest. Bart had commissioned it from a young sculptor, to rival the slightly more appropriate gargoyles atop the property next door. That house had belonged, 400 years earlier, to Jane Seymour, third wife of Henry VIII. Its gargoyles were not going to outdo Bart, who borrowed the stork motif from Holland, calling it a symbol of friendliness.

Bart had created a hybrid of Metro-Goldwyn Tudor – ornate, ersatz and flamboyant. The six-bedroomed mansion was a tin-pan Taj Mahal, dubbed Ye Olde Sunsette Boulevard by one visitor, tailor-made for the restless tycoon who chain-smoked and partied within its silken walls. Bart saw to it that he was ministered to constantly, employing a butler, a secretary, a chauffeur, a maid, a daily and a housekeeper. All this was for outward display – show business of a different kind. A granite-topped aquarium was a mock-granite- (actually fibre-glass-) topped aquarium. The mock-marble fruit bowl contained artificial cherries. Every niche was replete with genuine reproductions.

In all, there were twelve rooms (though some visitors recall twenty-five!) – including a Blue Room, a Black Room with one wall of black glass, a Lilac Room (now world famous) with its lilac bathroom and sunken bath, and an Indian Room – rooms for every mood, plus dozens of nooks and crannies, a roof garden, a full-size cinema and sound-proofing throughout. Each of the twelve rooms had its own telephone, five contained TV sets. Principal among them was the 35-foot-square Gothic Hall, with Bart's bedroom on the minstrel gallery, once described as displaying taste which vacillated between the Battle of Agincourt (one wall was a hand-painted mural of the subject) and *Modesty Blaise*. It featured two vast chandeliers copied from those in Canterbury Cathedral which had been made for the film *Becket* and came in a job lot of other props and fixtures which Bart had subsequently purchased for well over their non-existent value. The hall's floors were scattered with animal skins, its windows draped like a Plantagenet tent, its ceiling a harmony of cream and gold. Most visited perhaps – certainly most talked about – were the sauna lined with Californian pine (which could only be reached by the initiated through a secret back passage) and the Gothic throne room with its high-backed dark wooden ecclesiastical commode and lavatory-paper holder playing Handel's *Water Music*. A door grille like that in a confessional enabled the pressured mogul to communicate with others even during the wasted minutes of evacuation, much in the manner of President Johnson and the recently deceased Sir Winston Churchill. Another lavatory was a simple rectangle lined entirely with dark mirror-glass, and equipped with silver dolphin-shaped taps.

The master bedroom, overlooking the constant merrymaking in the main hall, was a toyshop of electronic gizmos, installed long before Stirling Moss or Sir Clive Sinclair had wired themselves for action. From a switch-pad by the bed (itself covered in a rust-coloured bedspread entirely hand-knitted by the housekeeper Bart had since thoughtfully retired) the fun-loving party-giver could raise a purple curtain, revealing the party-goers below. When the amusement flagged, another button changed the record on the stereo, lowered a cinema screen (first a square one, then Cinemascope) or ejected a television set from the wall. And, when it all got *too* much, Bart could find peace in a secluded, antique panelled study with its crystal-filled display cabinet, where he would not even be disturbed by a ringing phone. On the dado a pin-prick of green light would flash discreetly to tell him he was wanted on the line by his secretary. The only pictures were of the Artful Dodger, Noël Coward and Napoleon. Behind the desk, Lionel reigned in his deep, winged armchair.

Bart, the last son of an Austrian immigrant tailor, had become his own creation, a Chelsea replica of Kubla Khan in his pleasure-dome of mock treasures surrounded by mock friends. And who were the passing throng helping themselves to the cash placed in glasses on the mantelpiece or to the piles of hash around the coffee tables, or to triples of anything from Islay malts to blue Curaçao in the well-stocked bar? Lionel never tires of telling the story of how Paul McCartney 'just dropped in', hummed a theme and asked what the country's greatest living composer (who still couldn't write a note) thought of it. The theme was 'Yesterday'.[6] Neither can he resist reminding any passing audience that Michael Caine and Terence Stamp camped there 'when they didn't have the price of a breakfast of scrambled eggs' – though why they should have required their eggs scrambled is never explained. On one occasion, Glenys Roberts recalls, 'the elegant double doors were opened by his man Tony, and there, sprawled on the black leather studio couch, was Terence Stamp, looking like an ancient Greek ploughboy. Next to him was an actor called Ben

Carruthers – both of them in exotic Oriental costumes, and a girl who said she was sometimes Pamela and sometimes Judy.' In the mid-sixties it was what passed for normality among the 'theatrical set'.

And let no one forget the constant ins and outs of the pretty things and the folk heroes, like the Rolling Stones, whose manager Andrew Oldham was still forever planning new ventures with Bart. In some ways the open-house was becoming a Swinging Sixties precursor of Andy's Factory. Alma, Georgia, Brian, Noël and John were among the regulars (Cogan, Brown, Epstein, Coward, Lennon were the surnames it was unnecessary – and infra dig – to drop). Justin de Villeneuve showed off his new discovery Twiggy. Rising pop bands plonked out their compositions on the piano or the hand-painted clavichord (which Bart has to this day). Julie Driscoll happened by one day...and stayed for six months. Harebrained schemes came and went like bad trips – for example, 'Choosies', which now seems as outlandish as a portable phone. This was Bart's screen invention whereby cinema audiences would change the action by pressing buttons on the seat in front of them – giving options like 'comedy' or 'romance'. Or there was the idea for the waterproof book – just the right length for a bathtime read, with pages that would float and not stick together.

Bart was a notorious night-bird. The Fun Palace was just that – a place where fun could be had at any time of the day or, more usually, of the night; a place where the 1966 World Cup-winning squad had their post-match party; where wads of tenners were on display for the needy to help themselves to, or for guests flamboyantly to throw a lighted match into, as proof of their disdain for the stuff. These were the days when the sixties generation experimented with this or that latest amphetamine: pep pills, purple hearts, mandies, speed. Yet there was a downside, according to Victor Spinetti:[7] 'I saw people playing poker with him when he was drunk, and not scrupling to take his money. There were bets struck of £30,000, and Lionel would pay up. I couldn't bear it – to see people taking advantage of Lionel's hospitality when he was completely out of it. With the Beatles, I saw that in the middle of the huge entourage surrounding them there was a still, small centre. But in the middle of Lionel's hangers-on there was just Lionel having a ball. He told me that he'd decided to stop when he was rudely awakened one morning by something falling heavily on his face. He had crashed out on the floor by the front door, and this was the mail coming through the letter-box.' Then there were the hugely inflated bills at restaurants such as the Black Angus and clubs like the Pickwick, where Lionel was presented with £300 or £400 tabs, and unquestioningly paid them in cash.

Trying to tread water in this whirlpool was impossible, so Bart found himself a fashionable guru and took up yoga. His Indian mentor taught him that everyone has a 'sound' which is 'biologically and psychologically you'. Once found, the sound must never be disclosed, but it was without doubt based on the familiar 'omm' which, combined with a darkened room for twenty minutes, could provide a short recuperative period. The yoga would certainly help Bart cope with the pressure he was beginning to feel from the constant plague of 'knockers'.

Such ostentatious revelry brings a poignant irony to a court case that Lionel was in the process of pursuing against a council planning application. Through his solicitor, Mr David Jacobs, an appeal was made at a pubic inquiry on 10 August 1965 in Kensington Town Hall, at that time situated opposite Barkers in Kensington High Street. The inquiry was told that if a fourth-floor studio was allowed to be put up in Fulham Road above a parade of shops, the house in Seymour Walk would be in full view of the studio's occupants. The solicitor's argument was that 'Lionel Bart is an international personality, and people in that category find it most difficult to obtain accommodation suitable for their privacy. He went to infinite time and trouble before going to Seymour Walk, and spent a vast sum of money on the house. He built a trellis fence round the garden in an effort to get privacy – this will ruin it. He is visited constantly by high figures including members of the royal family, so he wishes to preserve his privacy.' Certainly, it was one among many reasons why privacy should be paramount.

But when Bart really desired privacy, he could find it a three-hour flight away in Morocco, where he had recently begun to rent a property in the Tangier Casbah. York Castle had been acquired in the 1930s by a real-estate company belonging to the fourth Marquess of Bute, who had discovered on its walls drawings made by prisoners in the late seventeenth century. Bart himself may have been intrigued by the story that the Castle had secret passageways linked to a network of tunnels under the Casbah, and decided to rent the retreat from its owner, the French interior designer Yves Vidal, on the understanding that its sitting tenant (an American writer) could remain. For privacy, Lionel arranged to have a set of keys to the neighbouring hotel, where he could escape if necessary from the throngs of English like Joe Orton, Kenneth Williams and others, for whom North Africa had become the anything-goes Mediterranean playground.

The story of Lionel Bart from this point forward is not one of decline and fall. Rather, it is fall and decline. Almost like a wound, the shock and lingering memory of *Twang!!* was to remain open, suppurating and draining Bart of any creative lifeblood he might have left in him. His pain turned quickly to anger. He began to knock the knockers. He blamed 'them' for the failure of *Twang!!* – 'them' being the unnamed members of a showbusiness cartel running the theatres, the television networks and the ticket agencies. 'The problems of the creative group – Joan Littlewood and so on – were a small factor, something that could have been overcome. And the criticisms in the newspapers were a small factor that could have been overcome...as in fact they have been in the past when public opinion has rallied round something it liked. My battle has not been to save a so-called artistic flop, it's been a battle against the combined giants of showbusiness in this country. I want to let off steam on this. I want to remain independent. I don't want a guv'nor. I've been grafting for eight years. I'd rather have freedom. I've grown tired of doing battle with *them*, within the nasty mundane politics that exist. Only a few can stand up to *them* in this town. There's myself. There's Brian Epstein. But my inclination is to get out of it.' And in the next breath, he announced that *Twang!!* was to go to Broadway. It didn't.

All right, so 'Living Doll' was one of the few British songs to make the American hit parade, but Bart was now being regularly attacked for plagiarism. His tastes were constantly criticized. His dress sense was erratic, even at a time when women were wearing broad belts and calling them microskirts. 'I dress to be different, but only because I don't want to conform to a set of rules from the past. I want it to be either contemporary or part of the future.' He refused to prove that he knew what 'good taste' was, and started trumpeting his own taste for kitsch. He began to be proud of being the amateur who had left school at thirteen, and who was still unable to write a note of music. 'They say I pinch other people's tunes. Certainly I'm subconsciously influenced by what has been written in the past. But who isn't? So even if I have written a couple of songs that might sound reminiscent, that's not many in a list of nearly 2,000[8]...some of which have made people's reputations. It all boils down to the fact that the knockers resent my lack of academic training. On paper, I couldn't tell you the difference between an A-flat and a council house.'

Unrepentantly (and, some have said, uncharacteristically), Noël Coward continued to be mad about the boy, and went on record to defend the millionaire who had made his fortune and fame more by his wits than by his talents. As the Master proudly said in October 1966: 'I'd rather spend five minutes in a four-ale bar chatting with Lionel Bart than a year's yachting cruise with the Oxford Debating Society.' But friends and former allies were finding it increasingly tiresome to put up with Lionel's little moments – moments of aggression, of self-esteem gone wild, of depression, of reluctance to deal with the real world – probably the one contributing factor to the decline which persists thirty years later. Even in 1967 the press was asking, in a *Daily Mirror* headline of 3 August: 'WHATEVER HAPPENED TO LIONEL BART?' It is perhaps worth quoting the newspaper's answer.

There was a time when the magic of song writer Lionel Bart sparkled from our hit parade. But not any more.

It's over three years since a Bart composition appeared in the charts. Since the crash of his last musical *Twang!!* eighteen months ago, little has been heard of him.

And when I looked him up this week – coincidentally on his thirty-seventh birthday – he tipped his Spanish sombrero back on his head, grinned and told me: 'I've been a hermit, man, for the past two years.'

But behind the grin was a lot of anger and frustration. For Bart is finding it impossible to boost his new, gigantic musical, _The Hunchback of Notre Dame_, off the launching pad.

'It's taken me five years to write and will maybe take another five years to get on,' he sighed. 'Almost every producer in the world is scared of it.'

Bart insists that this is not because _Twang!!_ folded.

'Remember I had five hit musicals before then – but _Hunchback_ is probably the most spectacular conception for the stage ever dreamed of.'

And he added: 'Maybe they'll put the show on after I die and then realise what a winner it is.'

And he paced the floor of his castle-like pad in Chelsea, which he is putting up for sale at around £100,000.

'What's the point in staying here?' he said. 'A bachelor in a six-bed-roomed house?

'Besides, unless I move the hippies will be making this their head-quarters.

'I'm getting besieged by the flower people and when I wake up some mornings I don't recognize some of the faces still hanging around...'

Speculation about those wild nights at the Fun Palace is as near as we'll ever come to the true picture: even those who were there find it hard to recall exactly what went down in the smog of uppers, downers, side-winders, cocaine, grass and gin, created by assorted freeloaders. Those journalists who managed to corner the normally effusive and ebullient Cockney were now reporting that they found him 'subdued' – usually a euphemism for hung-over. True, Bart still had his dreams and projects: he was to appear in a film called _The Touchables_ which Robert Freeman was to direct in Britain. Bart was to play the manager of a teenage idol who is kidnapped.[9] José Ferrer and Terence Stamp were said to be inter-ested in playing the _Hunchback_...or was it to be called _Quasimodo?_ – either way, it was now referred to as an 'opera' since it was devoid of dia-logue. Then, of course, there was the Hollywood movie score for _Gulliver's Travels_, and an offer from New York to write a television spe-cial for Carol Channing. There was his own life-story captured on vinyl

– Decca Records appear to have given him unlimited studio time for what was arguably the first concept-album, *Isn't This Where We Came In?*, scheduled to include a cast of over 2,000 performers, among them: several symphony orchestras, two Guards bands, the Dagenham Girl Pipers, Dusty Springfield playing the spoons, Bart's 'daily' with the single line of dialogue 'Oh, my Gawd', and Bart himself singing a dozen songs. The second track is a song inside the womb: 'then you feel you're being born. A lot of it is very wistful and sad, but it's basically happy: everyone is going to think we've all got something in common.' Another of the songs is called 'Throwaway Collapsible Soapbox', and one forgettable track is about George Alfred Blake working in an employment exchange. As for the appropriate 'vocal bag' for himself, Lionel was forced to admit defeat. 'I've done thousands of demonstration discs showing artists how I want my songs sung, and I've always tried to sound like them – Anthony Newley, Shirley Bassey, Louis Armstrong. When I tried to sound like myself, it was like a cross between Bud Flanagan and Donovan.' The sleeve was to be either a mirror or a blank sheet of music, on which would-be songwriters could put down their own compositions, with the best to be honoured by being recorded on Bart's next album! And in his *News of the World* column 'Alan Freeman Talks Pop', dear old Fluff was letting his readers in on another 'sinful Soho' exclusive: Bart and ex-Searcher Chris Curtis, now a record-producer himself, were making an audience-participation LP. Bart, inventor of karaoke? It seems so. If Fluff is to be believed, the notion was: 'you play the record, and join in'. And his final verdict on his old mate? 'That boy certainly has ideas!' And some of them above his station.

At the end of 1967 Bertrand Russell wrote to Lionel Bart, saying how enthusiastic he was at the prospect of Mr Bart turning his early book *Satan in the Suburbs* into a musical. Mr Bart was equally pleased to have such a nice letter of approval from Lord Russell, boasting that one of the greatest minds in the world wanted to work with him. And, what's more, they were to have a 'session' together on it soon. The idea of a collaboration between the author of *Principia Mathematica* and the creator of *Twang!!*, far-fetched though it might appear, was Russell's own. The veteran scientist and philosopher had first written to Bart with his suggestion in 1964, when he was already ninety-two. It seems the two of them discussed the matter over the phone several times, prompting Bart to order all Russell's books – with which he was totally unfamiliar – from Foyle's. 'They arrived...a whole truckload of them. I thought, God, nobody could be this prolific.' Taking Russell's first published excursion into fiction, Bart set out to master the short-story collection *Satan in the Suburbs*, published in 1953 when the author was already in his eightieth year. But, even after several attempts, Lionel remained baffled: 'I could not get to grips with it. Basically, it had already been done as a musical: *Damn Yankees!* has the same kind of plot.' And was Russell really that keen? 'It went back several years for him, and he really wanted to do something new. I was knocked out that he asked me, and tremendously impressed that a man of that age should want to play new games. It made me very proud that such a great head wanted to work with me. He said he admired some of my work, but he wasn't so silly as to say particularly what.' Sadly, the outcome of the collaboration will never be known. Bertrand Russell's death in 1970 extinguished all chance of one of the strangest musical partnerships ever imagined.

With a nod in the direction of *My Fair Lady,* Lionel next set his sights on Bernard Shaw's *St Joan* as a suitable candidate for canonization in a gospel musical with Madeline Bell. The Shaw estate was, reputedly, a little chary. What matter? Lionel was in the middle of writing *another* musical, this one with the American Charles K. Peck, Jr (who, ten years earlier, had sunk Maureen O'Hara in a show he co-authored with Pearl S. Buck, called *Christine*). This was the stage adaptation of Federico Fellini's 1954 film *La Strada*. Cy Coleman had found instant success with *Sweet Charity*, a musical based on Fellini's *Nights of Cabiria*, just as *9* was to strike the same vein of gold as the moviemaker's *8½*. But Bart was beset by personal demons. His Midas touch had already deserted him. It was just taking a while for the Americans to tune in to the fact. In the summer of '67 he was predicting the show would open in September '68. In August '68 he was planning to start rehearsals on Broadway in November, and searching for a leading-lady to take the famous Giulietta Massina part, someone with 'that marvellous clown quality and able to dance and sing, with the range of, say Streisand'. He did try Streisand, 'but she's tied up for four movies, darling, at $1 million a shot'. An expensive demo disc was pressed for backers, featuring, instead of Barbra, Madeline Bell, the Mike Sammes Singers and a twenty-five-piece orchestra. Yul Brynner, Marlon Brando, Topol and Anthony Quinn were all said to be interested in the lead role of Zampano, the insanely jealous circus strong-man. In fact, none of them was in the cast or even the audience when _La Strada_ hit the Broadway stage – with a massive resounding thud – on 14 December 1969 at the Lunt-Fontanne Theatre, New York. It closed at the same theatre on 15 December 1969.

Bart's was the only 'name' attached to the project. Yet during the out-of-town try-out his score was gradually removed until, on opening night, only three of his songs remained. In the playbill there was a special insert, which read: 'At this performance, additional music and lyrics by Martin Charnin and Elliot Lawrence.' It was, in effect, an entirely new score. Yet neither its new music nor some numbers which sounded uncannily in the style of Bart, could stop the show from losing $650,000 in a spectacular one-night stand. Because it slavishly followed the film's screenplay of circus jealousies and deaths, _La Strada_ was panned as one of the most depressing musicals ever written. Sadly for her, its female lead was Bernadette Peters, whose career was probably held back by several years because of the show's instant failure.

It was not the only setback that year. Nor the only one that could be blamed on Bart's infatuation with Broadway. In the early hours of 16 May 1969 a charming young man in a floral cravat met the police at the door of Bart's mansion in Seymour Walk. They had raced there as a result of telephone call. The young man told the three constables that he was a friend. 'I'm just leaving,' he announced to them, 'I have a key...I'll let you in.' And in a scene reminiscent of an Ealing Comedy, he did just that. The policemen entered to discover the place in a shambles. Many of Bart's precious, if tasteless, possessions were missing. And so, they soon found out, was the charming young man in the floral cravat. A few minutes later Bart's housekeeper Alec Payne arrived at the house to itemize exactly what had gone: Bart's favourite painting (the military portrait of Napoleon), a chiming clock with theatrical figures given to Bart for his birthday the previous year, a safe which was hidden in a cupboard and bolted to the ground, several antiques, a television set, two film projectors and some silver. The total loss and damage (including a thirteenth-century two-handed sword which had been bent) was calculated at around £2,000.

Apparently, the thieves had spent most of the night inside the house, drinking bottles of whisky and other spirits from the bar as they went about their business of completely ransacking the unsaleable home. It looked as though they had climbed over a glass canopy on the extension to the building, letting themselves in by breaking a glass panel. Yet peculiarly, no alarm went off at the time, despite almost every window and door being wired. As Mr Payne himself said: 'I defy anyone who has not been in this house before to walk ten paces without setting off that alarm.' How prophetic his judgment was to prove...

And that young man in the floral cravat? A Scotland Yard spokesman overcame any embarrassment to admit: 'A man was seen on the premises and gave what seemed to be a satisfactory explanation. After he had been allowed to go, it was decided the explanation was not really satisfactory.'

When the case came to court at the end of October, in the dock was long-haired Anthony Haydon, aged twenty-one, unemployed and of no fixed address, who pleaded not guilty to the theft at Bart's home. Called as a prosecution witness, Bart arrived at the court in a new, chauffeur-driven Daimler. In evidence, he agreed that he had rung Haydon, and told him he did not believe he had committed the vandalism, pleading with the young man to go to the police and protest his innocence. Bart said he knew Haydon (who was an orphan) as a friend initially. The accused had worked for him in the past and had also been a travelling companion. He had, in fact, known Lionel for some years, and lived with him at the house for several periods, the first occasion being for two or three months in 1967. When asked by the defence counsel whether Mr Bart ever entrusted things to him, Mr Haydon replied: 'Yes, everything.' He said he handled money for the composer and collected Bart's weekly allowance from his accountants. Denying the theft, he said: 'I could not bring myself to do such a thing. Lionel is a very great friend of mine. There would be no reason at all for doing it.'

It was hardly the kind of publicity Lionel needed. And, exacerbating the proceedings, he himself incurred the bench's ire by protesting the youth's innocence. Judge Murray Buttrose suddenly silenced the hearing at the Inner London Sessions with the following outburst against Haydon's defending barrister, Mr John Samuels: 'I don't care two hoots what Mr Bart thinks. What he says is absolutely irrelevant. Are you asking that Mr Bart should supersede the jury? Mr Bart is not the judge nor the jury in this case. The jury will decide in this matter, not Mr Bart. The fact that Lionel Bart thinks the accused did not commit the robbery is completely irrelevant. He was in America when this happened. He employed this man for a short time, and this was a long time before the offence occurred. He does not know the facts except that it is a friend and erstwhile employee who is accused. I shall tell the jury firmly and categorically that whether they think the defendant had committed the offence has nothing to do with Mr Bart.'

The courtroom was hushed. And, for a rare moment, so was Lionel. Haydon was also denying charges of breaking into two other houses and stealing a total of £4,500 in cash and jewellery, as well as dishonestly handling thirteen luncheon vouchers – total value, say, 49 pence. In his evidence, Haydon claimed he was at a club in Soho on the night of the robbery. For the prosecution, Police Constable L. Spence said that in the early hours of 16 May he saw his fellow police officers at the open front door to Bart's house, where they were talking with a man whom he recognized as Haydon. When he went into the house, he found there was 'quite a lot of disorder'. On 22 October 1969 Judge Buttrose told Haydon that he had been convicted of 'major burglaries'. He had six previous convictions, and was remanded until the end of the month for further inquiries.

In the months between the burglary and the court hearing, Bart had finally managed to sell the Fun Palace, for a reputed £100,000, to 'an American connected with the film industry'. He returned to the flat in Reece Mews, although newspaper reports had him looking for a house in Dublin, where he had spent the ten days immediately prior to the trial, in search of some peace and quiet. According to his manager

Stephen Komlosy, it would once again be something special: 'I'm too scared to say how much he intends to spend on this one in Dublin. But, you know it's going to be pretty lavish.'

As the new decade dawned with its promises of platform shoes, 5-inch lapels and 26-inch bell-bottoms, Bart's star looked to any amateur astrologer to be unmistakably in the descendant. In the second week of January Bart's Bentley was stopped in Albemarle Street, just off Piccadilly, with Bart at the wheel. When he appeared at Bow Street magistrates' court on 5 February 1970, he elected to go for trial on a charge of being unfit to drive through drink or drugs, and was allowed bail in his own recognizance of £50. At the hearing on 27 May, he was described by the police as 'meandering gently from side to side of the road'. He was also travelling in the wrong direction down a one-way street. Bart was given a breath-test which showed positive. A blood test at the police station showed no alcohol, but he was judged 'unfit to drive' by the doctor on duty, Dr John Gavin. In his defence, Lionel explained that he had been in America for nine months immediately prior to the incident, and that even the policeman 'would have made the same mistake'. Wearing a gold velvet suit, massive kipper tie and white suede boots, Bart told the court of a night out on the town with Sean Kenny. After a meal of mussels and spaghetti in an Italian restaurant in Knightsbridge, they went to a Mayfair club for a nightcap. Afterwards, he arranged to drive Kenny and another friend home to Chelsea, and agreed to give a lift to another couple who lived near him.

'Those two had been drinking heavily and were very, very tipsy. I had four backseat drivers. They were all giving directions on which was the best way to get down near the river.' As he approached Piccadilly, he turned round to tell them to be quiet, and accidentally turned right instead of left. 'Everyone in the car was shouting at the same time. It was chaotic. I decided it was best to stop and calm them down, which I was doing when the police stopped me.' Bart admitted that he might have appeared slightly drunk to the police officer, as earlier in the day he had taken strong decongestant tablets, and had been injected with methedrine by his doctor because of tiredness and depression. His evidence continued: 'I have a broken nose and suffer badly from chest and nasal congestion. I had been working very hard for the past two days, barely having a couple of hours' sleep. I was working on a new show with Sean.'

The case continued the following day, with yet another curious warning from the judge, this time His Honour David John Stinson, who told the jury of ten men and two women not to be swayed by Bart's fame in arriving at their verdict. 'You may feel in a little difficulty in dealing with somebody about whom you know something. Everybody knows who Lionel Bart is and what he does. We are beyond the age when a judge might lean forward and say "Who is Lionel Bart?" But Mr Bart is entitled to be considered as dispassionately as any other defendant. It just happens that he is gifted with genius, and seems to live the kind of life many of us would think impossible. But Mr Bart is obliged to conform to the laws of the land. Don't say "I could not possibly convict this nice Mr Bart who writes such lovely songs."' Bart's defence was in the hands of Michael Havers, QC, the future Attorney-General and father of actor Nigel. He told the jury that 'things ain't what they used to be for the motorist'. And, explaining Lionel's need to take antihistamine to relieve congestion, added: 'The word drug has a dirty connotation these days. This was an ordinary hay fever drug for people who suffer from congestion.'

The jury cleared Bart of the charge. Outside the court, an oversize homburg covering his tumbling, shoulder-length black curls, the 'genius' breathed in the air of a free man. 'It's been a fair deal all round. I am very happy. I was inspired last night and wrote my song "Just Give 'em Time" after yesterday's hearing. I sat up in bed all night working on the new show *Gulliver's Travels*. Now I can get back to it without this weight hanging over me.'

At his next court appearance, he was not going to get off so lightly.

CHAPTER SEVEN

I'D DO ANYTHING

'PETER SELLERS TO BE FAGIN IN *OLIVER!* FILM.' With the assurance and authority usually found in that newspaper, the *Daily Telegraph*'s 'own correspondent' in New York delivered to its readers the copper-bottomed truth in a three-paragraph story on the morning of 17 April 1964. Within two months, those dedicated patrician readers would savour at least twenty times more column inches under the more partial headline, 'LIONEL BART SUED OVER *OLIVER!* FILM'.[1] What had gone wrong...again?

From the moment of its bouncing birth in June 1960, it was clear that *Oliver!* would follow a path worn by *Oklahoma!, Carousel, South Pacific* and more, and ultimately find its way on to celluloid. Quite how, when, with whom and by whom were questions which arose periodically from that day onwards. All would be answered by Lionel, and Lionel alone would be responsible for answering them, since Lionel had ensured he had total control over every aspect of casting, from the director down. And Lionel nurtured names for each of the principal roles – often a little too publicly. Among the first in the frame for Fagin was Peter O'Toole, who in 1962 became all-conquering mystical hero as *Lawrence of Arabia*.

Bart, however, received a telephone call from Peter Sellers, making a case for his own interpretation as far better than O'Toole's. Easily convinced, Bart concurred, agent talked unto agent, and lo the Columbia Pictures company spake to the press, pointing out that the film was to be made for Columbia by Brookfield Productions, 'a company owned jointly by Mr Sellers and John Bryan, who will be the producer for this picture. The director has not yet been selected.'[2] That simple announcement led to a cooling off between O'Toole and Bart that lasted some years. But Bart was not inwardly as convinced as he had outwardly revealed himself to be. And part of the reason lay in the *Telegraph*'s final paragraph: 'This will be the first film that Mr Sellers will make after his recovery from his recent serious heart attack.' Considerable doubts over his health led to Lionel re-entering talks and negotiations with Laurence Olivier, with Danny Kaye, with Richard Burton, who was also up to play Sikes alongside the only possible Nancy – Elizabeth Taylor. (Lionel often retells a dainty story of Liz locking him in one of the lavatories in his Seymour Walk mansion while she sings for him 'As Long As He Needs Me'.)

Bart, in effect, was being accused of wanting only 'his own pet producer and star actor' in the screen version of *Oliver!* and was being sued over the issue of casting. Lionel wanted the film to be made by Brookfield Productions, because this would guarantee the appearance of Peter Sellers as Fagin. By the time the case was heard, Sellers was in Los Angeles, but swore an affidavit, in which he claims he would be happy to play Fagin in a Brookfield film, but not in one made by Romulus Films, the first choice of Donmar Productions[3] to make the movie. And, to tip the scales of justice in his and Bart's favour, Sellers had his doctors issue a statement confirming that he would be fit to resume work by September or October, and would be well enough to make a film such as *Oliver!* Bart himself weighed in with a declaration of 'no confidence' in the ability of Romulus to produce the film to the same artistic standards as Brookfield, but his sense of outrage was diluted with the revelation in court that Brookfield was nothing more than a private company,[4] which had never produced any film, with a paid-up share capital of £2. How then had it managed to offer £143,000[5] for the world picture rights to the show? According to their defence, the offer was guaranteed by the Columbia Picture Corporation on condition that Sellers and only Sellers would play Fagin. Sir Andrew Clark, QC, for Donmar, counterclaimed that there was no sort of guarantee that Peter Sellers would be available, so Columbia's guarantee was really worthless. What Donmar was seeking was to have an injunction issued against Lionel Bart[6] restraining him from disposing of the world film, television and radio rights, except to Romulus Films, who had put in a counter-offer of £150,000,[7] and had acted by immediately issuing a cheque for £89,000. They had offered Bart himself an additional £37,500[8] for his services as collaborator on the picture and for writing new music if required, as against the original offer of £33,300[9] by Brookfield. They had even offered to employ Sellers, if he were available.

Under an agreement made in May 1959, when Donald Albery bought the rights to *Oliver!*, the contract stated that Donmar were entitled to 40 per cent of the proceeds received by Lionel Bart of any disposal of the film, radio or commercial TV rights, in return for which Donmar had agreed to present the play in London and New York – as they had now done. The vital clause in that agreement details that if Bart received a bona fide offer for the motion picture rights, he should immediately notify Donmar of such an offer, and if such offer should be unacceptable to them, they should within ten days of notification either submit a better bona fide counter-offer from a third party, or themselves offer to purchase the world rights on the same terms as the original offer, and that Lionel would be bound to accept such an offer, but in default of the Donmar counter-offer, he would be free either to accept or refuse the original offer. Romulus was a well-known, well-respected film company with successes like *The Pumpkin Eater*, *Moulin Rouge* and *Room at the Top* to its credit. Why was Bart being untrue to himself in accepting the lower offer? Why, moreover, was he apparently reneging on the contract he had signed with the only person who showed an interest in *Oliver!* five years earlier? Partly, the higher offer meant he was being bought out of total control – which, to many in the business who knew his ways in those days, could mean total irreconcilable interference. Partly, it was a sincere desire to see Sellers in the role of the Jewish mother-hen, with all the international status his name on the billing could then command. And why was Donmar so keen on Romulus, despite Brookfield's subsequent offer to match the Romulus offer? Was it that they might lose the benefit of an agreement with Romulus to share 50–50 (as opposed to the existing 40–60) any profits accruing from the exploitation of the rights?

A High Court slanging match began with Donmar's counsel claiming that Bart had been discovered and made by Albery's faith in *Oliver!* In a feisty retort, Mr A. J. Balcombe claimed that a remark of this nature was not only damaging to a person in Bart's position, it was 'quite incorrect', as Bart had written or co-written *Lock Up Your Daughters, Fings* 'and several popular songs and music for films, including *Tommy the Toreador* and *The Tommy Steele Story*'. By way of response Donmar's brief, Sir Andrew Clark, assured the court that Romulus Films Ltd would have no difficulty securing a distribution agreement with a major American distributor, and that Romulus did 'not accept that Peter Sellers was the only actor who could play the role of Fagin. That role could be performed by such stars as Sir Laurence Olivier, Sir Alec Guinness,[10] Sir Ralph Richardson, Danny Kaye, Kirk Douglas, Peter O'Toole and Laurence Harvey.' At issue, simply, was the question of what exactly constituted a 'better offer'. Better financially? Better artistically? Better in the long term? Better for one party or both parties? The original agreement, quite definitively, gave no right to Lionel to decide who should produce the film. If he rejected the better financial offer, he would be in breach of that agreement. He was now arguing that that offer would *not* be better for the only person whose position was at stake – the author. Apart from his doubts about distribution and casting, Bart's QC, Mr J. T. Moloney was now introducing into the equation his client's deeper, intangible concerns, which went far beyond any money he might earn from the project. Bart, he argued, was also entitled to take into account with whom he would have to collaborate in the film production, 'that is to say, the harmonious personal relationship in the implementation of the film plan is very important. The author must have his own ideas how his artistic values are represented to the public.'

And another factor was brought into play late that afternoon, as though neither side had been remotely aware of the urgency of concluding the hearing. Bart's preferred Brookfield offer was due to expire the next day, and he had no guarantee (according to his lawyers) that it would be renewed. Would the Donmar–Romulus bid also be allowed to expire, leaving Bart with the possibility of nobody being interested in the film rights? The very idea! But, in an exemplary haste to see justice done – at least for the time being – by day three the judge, Mr Justice Ungoed-Thomas, was ready to make his ruling. He issued a temporary injunction, preventing Bart from trying to dispose of the rights and preventing Brookfield from taking part in any dealings in the film copyright until the case was heard in full four months hence. He then ruled that 'better offer' was deemed only to mean better 'in a financial sense without concerning with Mr Bart's reaction to it. And on that basis it is immaterial whether better meant for Mr Bart only or for both the parties.' And, acting as judge and film jury, he added that the Peter Sellers factor did not necessarily make the Brookfield offer any better than the one made by Romulus. Bart was a little less than delighted by this outcome. The film was eventually produced by Romulus...and Columbia Pictures.

Not that the lesser parts were proving any simpler to allot or adjudicate over. With filming due to begin at Shepperton Studios in June 1967, the last weeks of 1966 were spent considering applications from over 2,000 boys, some from parts of the Commonwealth as remote as Australia. Romulus had to employ 'four girls' at their Park Lane offices, solely to deal with replies prior to the auditions in the new year, when the search would officially start for a small boy with angelic looks to match those of John Howard Davies, star of David Lean's 1948 movie. In the event Mark Lester,[11] who was eight, proved to have the looks though not quite the talent: he spends the film bewildered and simpering. And who could play that cocky blend of fifteen-year-old kid and wise old man that made up Dodger? Davy Jones, Phil Collins and Steve Marriott, who were among the dozens who by now had shared the role on stage, were getting too long in the tooth to be winsome rogues, if not to be wanton rock stars. Jack Wild[12] easily lived up to his name, and is still grateful for the break it gave his career to have been discovered one day playing football by an agent. 'Looking back on it, it was really quite phenomenal, because one minute I could walk down the street with no trouble, and the next minute I was recognized everywhere I went. Life became much harder, but I still believe it's better to be known for something than for nothing.'

The film did not go into production until the summer of 1967, when Shepperton Studios, lying in sixty lush acres to the west of London, found themselves transformed into a Victorian underworld, a snowy street of bull's-eye-windowed shops or a Covent Garden plagued by swarms of singing, dancing costermongers. In fact, it remained thus transformed for over seven months, with only one scene (in which the young Oliver is covered in mud by a passing coach and horses while making his way to London) being shot outside the studio lot. Filming went on into the night and across every weekend. Budgets went soaring, and the backers became nervous, because for all that it could boast a cast of solid British repertory actors like Harry Secombe as Mr Bumble, Peggy Mount as Widow Corney, Leonard Rossiter, Hylda Baker and others, there was no international star, and the choice of director had surprised many.

Carol Reed had actually attempted to buy the film rights to *Oliver!* after seeing it on stage in 1960, but the price was beyond his reach. By 1967 he was no longer at the height of his powers, and had already caused raised eyebrows by casting his own nephew as Bill Sikes, though Carol Reed himself denied ever wanting Oliver Reed to play the thug. His views on casting were, however, generally heeded: he felt most strongly about Ron Moody, and convinced any doubters by repeatedly playing them the stage recording. Columbia for a long while remained unimpressed, and continued to favour Sellers, claiming that the film would need a star if it were to have any box office in the United States. Reed eventually had his way, though he was forced to concede to the American executives over the party of Nancy. The director badly wanted to cast Shirley Bassey. Columbia vetoed the choice, believing that US cinema-goers (especially in the South) would be offended by the murder of a black woman. Instead, the part went to a British cabaret performer, Shani Wallis. Moody, as expected, remains central to the

121

film, although the character is far less of an anti–Semitic stereotype than it was considered to be on stage. Wallis, however, was a major disappointment in the role of Nancy. In the final credits Bart's name appeared above the title, while Vernon Harris was credited as having written it.

When the film was released after its Royal Première in the presence of Princess Margaret at the end of September 1968, Barry Norman and Alexander Walker were among those who accorded it unanimous praise and endless superlatives. Walker's review begins: '*Oliver!* is a musical that couldn't give you a spoonful more if you got down on your knees and begged for it. It gives all it has got, and a tremendous amount of enjoyment that turns out to be....It represents the canonization of Mr Moody in theatrical history, the restoration of Sir Carol Reed to the top flight of film directors and the consummation of Lionel Bart – for unless they do *Oliver!* on ice (and knowing Mr Bart they very well may), what more can human ingenuity do to it?' Like Walker, Norman can find no fault with Ron Moody as Fagin, and leaves no room for even a flicker of speculation about what Sellers might have brought to the role. Moody's Fagin 'is a glorious creation, at once oily, villainous and lovable'. The last word goes to Ian Christie, writing in the *Sunday Express*: 'The film cost £4 million to make, and as far as I am concerned every penny was well spent. As far as musicals go this is exactly my bowl of gruel, a feast at which even Oliver himself couldn't ask for more.'

Lionel, however, could ask for more, and repeatedly did. Hollywood instantly began to woo him with seductive offers of 'total control', 'unsupervised budgets' and, the oldest and most alluring cliché of them all in Tinseltown – 'de luxe casting'. In March 1969, Lionel was packing to leave London for two years, having signed to Universal Pictures to write the music, lyrics and screenplay for musical versions of *Ruggles of Red Gap* and *Cyrano de Bergerac*. Bart was delighted by this sudden, enthusiastic recognition on the West Coast, which resulted entirely from the fact that he was about to collect six Academy Awards for the film of *Oliver!* 'At one time they seemed to regard me as a has-been. Sort of one half of Goldberg and Sullivan. But after the Hollywood première of *Oliver!* they wanted to give me the keys of the city.' In London Bart had the keys to, and was now driving, or being driven in, a Bentley Continental. A quiet holiday in Torquay meant renting an eight-room suite at the Imperial. A moment's mental arithmetic told him that, for the next decade, *Oliver!* alone would be earning him anything from £250,000 a year to an annual million. He might already have made and spent £4 million, though he hardly knew for sure. 'But I don't plan to die with any money in the bank. I am a compulsive spender. I've spent fortunes on cars, houses, booze and food.' If he needed a drink – and he now so frequently did – he had only to pick up the telephone on the sun terrace, and Alec, or another member of the household staff, would bring him two. Meals for a handful of close friends would often cost in excess of £100. At thirty-eight, he was still a bachelor...but rarely alone.

By the close of 1969 *Oliver!* was acknowledged as the most successful British film ever made. It had cost between £3 and £4 million to make, and in those first twelve months had enjoyed box-office returns of £20 million, and that amount came from only twenty-six cinemas out of 1,700 in Britain, and a couple of hundred out of several thousand in America. And its appeal was strikingly universal: in a rare achievement for a British film, it was decided in Moscow that *Oliver!* was suitable for Soviet audiences. The surprise at its sales was heightened by the fact that it was a musical, a genre in which British film-makers had an undistinguished record, and which had furthermore worried the producer John Woolf. Despite his track record with *Moulin Rouge* and *The African Queen*, he was nervously aware that 'after it was a hit on the stage in London and New York I would have looked a damned fool if it hadn't been a success on the screen'. With such apprehension behind him, Woolf was able to evaluate the share of fortune which was coming everyone's way. Mark Lester had been paid £5,000 for his title role, and now had film and TV contracts that would bring him £800,000 before he was sixteen. Jack Wild as Dodger had received £100 a week, and was now receiving the same amount daily by starring in an American television series and making eight guest appearances on the Rowan and Martin *Laugh In*. Lionel's cut was 10 per cent of the film's profits.

Meanwhile, by 1970 Hollywood had tired of Lionel sooner than Lionel had tired of Hollywood. His riproaring antics had included being driven everywhere in a convertible Cadillac, with as much respect given to his young, docile companion as to Bart himself. The youth was nicknamed Spencer Tracy, and the studio was more than happy to comply when Bart insisted on special notepaper for his chum. Spencer was Bart's inseparable, life-size teddy bear.

CHAPTER EIGHT

FINGS AIN'T WOT THEY USED T'BE

'LIONEL BART ARRESTED ON DRUGS CHARGE' screamed the one-inch-high letters across the front-page headline in the London *Evening Standard*. It was two days after Valentine's Day 1971 when Scotland Yard detectives raided Bart's home in Reece Mews, arrested 'the forty-year-old Cockney songwriter', drove him the half-mile to Chelsea police station and charged him with being in unauthorized possession of dangerous drugs. The officers removed from the flat 'substances which were later sent for analysis'. Bart was bailed to appear at Marlborough Street magistrates' court the next morning. That appearance, for which Lionel chose an unusually sober brown three-piece suit, blue shirt and dark kipper tie, lasted one minute, the time it took to remand him for a further three weeks until 9 March on his own recognizance of £100. The charge was now more detailed: he was accused of possessing cannabis resin 'without authority', though how and through whom such authority might be obtained has never been made clear in English jurisprudence. Bart left the court in the same chauffeur-driven Daimler which had brought him there.

When the case was eventually heard, the courtroom was told that it was Mr Bart's hospitality to others that had led to his appearance on a drugs charge, and that henceforward he intended to stop being so friendly to strangers because they took advantage of his hospitality. According to his solicitor, Mr Martin Polden, the ex-millionaire was 'not involved in the drug scene in dependence or addiction, nor is he any kind of advocate of it'. Which seemed a little hard to swallow when Mr R. B. Vince, prosecuting, told the court that at the time the police arrived at the flat, Bart agreed to a search and straight away handed over to them a box containing cannabis resin. And that, moreover, a metal pot containing a quantity of the drug and some joints ('cigarettes containing cannabis resin') were also found. Add to these certain other items which were subsequently analysed to show the possible presence of other drugs, and the evidence against him was beginning to look alarmingly conclusive. The police, however, were prepared to accept that Bart had no knowledge of the presence of these 'other substances', and Mr Polden insisted that, because Bart frequently allowed the flat to be used by strangers, the only possible explanation for the presence of cannabis was that it had been brought there during the owner's absence. Bart, appearing in court looking pug-like with half his face covered in mutton-chop whiskers and wearing a dark suit and green shirt topped off with a fawn-coloured fedora, had, however, pleaded guilty to the charge of possession of just under eight grams in total. In mitigation, his counsel argued: 'I would like to say something about the lifestyle of Mr Bart. It is Mr Bart's lot in life to have something of a generosity of spirit. It shows itself well in his plays and songs and in his theatrical life, but badly in its repercussions on his private life.' He went on to explain in heart-rending detail how Bart often gave hospitality to numbers of people, and that some who went to his flat were not known to him. The evening before the police arrived, some people asked to remain in the flat while he went out, and he agreed. When he returned the flat was deserted, 'and it was his particular misfortune that the police came the following morning. The cannabis had been brought in by someone else, but Bart knew it was there and told the police where it was. He does assure you that he is not involved in the drug scene, nor is he any kind of advocate for it.' In conclusion, Mr Polden affirmed that Bart intended to change his 'lifestyle' and pressed for a conditional discharge on the grounds that the cannabis had been brought to his flat by strangers, to which Mr St John Harmsworth, the magistrate, expressed his full sense of moral rectitude under threat: 'If I start conditionally discharging people, where is it going to end?' Around the time, many celebrities (especially in pop) were involved in drugs cases where they were convicted of possession only. Bart was fined £50 and ordered to pay £10 costs.

On 16 August 1968 Lionel Bart was telling David Wigg for his London *Evening News* 'Young Scene' interview (Lionel being a youthful thirty-eight at the time) that: 'It would be impossible for me to go completely bust, but I will never be a multi-millionaire, because I don't want to be... I've never been good with money. I have made and lost several fortunes.' If words were ever to haunt him, these would surely be the ones he heard over and over again on the morning of 29 February 1972 as he paid £10 over to the London Bankruptcy Court, just a five-shilling taxi ride from where his first hit *Fings* was staged, and filed his own petition in bankruptcy. The £10 was the cost of the receiving order made against him.

It was the beginning of a very long, messy ending for Bart. At the court he spent two hours with Mr Royston Howard, the senior examiner, explaining to whom he owed money, and the reasons why he was now unable to repay them. As in any case involving showbusiness copyrights and disputes, the facts are never simple and rarely emerge from the legal files of the parties involved. Two years earlier, in April 1970, Bart had been issued with a High Court writ by Peter Maurice Music Ltd,[1] music publishers, of Denmark Street, Soho. The company was claiming £36,068 in unpaid royalties on film and stage copyrights of *Oliver!* The company alleged that under a 1962 agreement disposing of a High Court action, it was to receive one fifth of all future royalties from the copyright in material written by Mr Bart for *Oliver!* and that it was to receive half-yearly accounts of all money received from the copyright. In the writ against Bart, against his company Lionel Bart Ltd and against Oliver Promotions of Chandos Street, Mayfair, the plaintiff Peter Maurice Music Ltd alleged that the defendants had 'persistently failed' to provide accounts under the agreement.

Emerging from the short hearing (which was to be followed by a public hearing later that month), Bart returned to his £5-a-week flat in Reece Mews, where he was making final amendments to *The Londoners*, another Cockney musical, this time based on the hit play by Stephen Lewis called *Sparrers Can't Sing*. It was due to open in less than a month – the first night was pencilled for 27 March at the Theatre Royal, Stratford, once home to Joan Littlewood, who was to return there to direct it. Although in no mood to provide his usual amount of copy to any waiting reporters, Bart did vouchsafe that he was going to have to work hard to pay off his creditors: 'I've been brought up not to run away from my own manor or welsh on debts – I'll do my damnedest to see everyone gets theirs.'

Under another complex arrangement in the network of companies set up to control and handle Bart's affairs, he was currently 'employed' by Tony de Fries, director of Classic Music Ltd. Though sympathetic to the plight of a man who had sold off his home for 'a pittance' (£100,000) to pay off a loan, and who had signed away his rights to *Oliver!* to meet other debts, Mr de Vries was correct in his early analysis that Bart's largest single creditor was likely to be, as it so often is in showbusiness careers, Her Majesty's Inspectorate of Taxes, the Inland Revenue. On 12 April 1972 a creditors' meeting in London was told that the taxman was owed an estimated £41,364 in income tax, surtax and capital gains tax, whereas the only assets disclosed by the 'music man' were £624 in cash and personal belongings. Truly a case of 'I, I Who Have Nothing'.

His total debts were put at £158,456, of which he expected only £96,066 to be claimed against him, and on these figures he was adjudged to be £95,442 in the red. Around a dozen creditors were told by Official Receiver Mr Royston Howard of a five-year agreement, signed only the previous year, giving the company Classic Music Ltd exclusive rights to Bart's income from songwriting. In return, he was receiving £300 a month 'to live on'. When one of the creditors wanted to know what could be done about that agreement, tied up in advance of the bankruptcy, the receiver promised it was something he would 'look into'. The question at issue was whether the creditors' rights over-rode any rights given by Bart before the bankruptcy. Bart, the while, waited in another room, and hurried away afterwards in a chauffeur-driven Ford car, teasing reporters with an unusually meagre five-word analysis: 'What can I say, boys?'

As the meeting was not a quorum, it had to be adjourned for a week. At this second meeting, on 19 April, the impresario Larry Parnes claimed he was owed £11,600. Subsequently, the creditors appointed Mr George Auger, an accountant, as trustee charged with trying to realize and distribute assets, though as a spokesman for Bart told him, 'Lionel does not have any hidden assets except his talent.' Yet that seemed to be ebbing away as fast as his invisible liquidity. As far as Bart was concerned, the business collapse could all be blamed on *Twang!!*, which had folded after four weeks. His companies borrowed £110,000 to launch it, and laid out another £20,000 on keeping its West End run afloat. Those monies had been repaid by signing away earlier creative rights (worth around £100,000 a year in the case of *Oliver!*) to the *Twang!!* backers. Then there was the company formed to acquire Bart a new house: £55,000 was spent on the property in Seymour Walk, West Brompton, with a further £140,000 needed to convert and furnish it, but which was eventually sold at a loss.

By day, he was watching from the sidelines as his fortunes were scrutinized by the law courts. By night, he was waiting in the wings as his theatrical fortunes were assessed by the theatre critics at Stratford East. *The Londoners* did open, as scheduled, on 27 March 1972. In the eighteen months since Joan Littlewood's last production at this venue, the surrounding landscape of pubs and little houses had been razed to a vast building site on which the citizens of Stratford would ultimately have a concrete-and-blight shopping precinct and office blocks. The theatre itself survived the carnage, and is still a quaint reminder of the way fings used t'be, stranded in Gerry Raffles Square, E15, like a Christmas tree in a bombsite. And within – an entertainment about back-garden community life in an area scheduled for the big lead ball: the story of Gran (played by Benny Hill's voluminous companion Rita Webb), who is moved out to a tower block, only to return after two days' isolation to barricade herself in her derelict end-of-terrace house. Lionel had not only written the music for the show, based on one of Joan's last successes during her legendary management at the Theatre Royal twelve years earlier; he was also appearing in it, unannounced towards the end, as a tearaway son released from prison. It was hardly deluxe casting for, as *The Times* pointed out:

> As Mr Bart patently would not harm a fly, his performance aptly rounds off the fairy tale....The show is more celebration than attack. And its real success is in creating theatrical situations from a group of people who are all likeable. Partly this is simply a matter of showing life going on: the lodger feeding his birds and the sex-starved widow dressing up to kill for a spiritualist seance: members of the Jugg family banging in and out of the outside lavatory with reading matter, and Mr Lewis himself pushing his battered pram around selling products that have been off the market for thirty years.

Although Bart's score was not entirely original (it included some old London standards) it appears never to have benefited from a professional recording. Nevertheless, on stage, full justice was done to the prolonged numbers by Bob Kerr's Whoopee Band on their traditional range of instruments: motor horns, saws, kazoos and teapots.

On 2 May disaster struck where the demolition man could not. Having taken over the role of the tramp, on his first night Lionel broke a bone in his foot and had to be taken to hospital after hobbling off stage. Just after the opening of the second act, he had had to go through a bedroom wall, but fell badly and staggered out in front of everybody mumbling about his ankle, before limping off. The audience seemed unaware of the division between dissembling and dislocating, and Mr Swithin Fry of East Ham, who was in the stalls, commented: 'It was very well done. Nobody would have known he was injured.' And how impertinently art was imitating life. Bart was being paid £25 a week as a performer in the same theatre which had housed his first musical success *Fings* just fifteen years earlier – and playing a destitute tramp, pushing his pram with the slogan WIFE & SMALL FAMILEE TO SUPPORT. If the tax man had a sense of humour, he would have smiled at the appropriateness of the image he was helping to authenticate.

130

Typically, Bart seemed far from downhearted, boasting that the future was looking rosy, that he was writing a double album of music for *The Hunchback of Notre Dame* (that immovable hump of a project), that Kirk Douglas had asked him to write music for the film *Scalawag*[2] and that he had been offered an enormous sum for the rights to *Maggie May*, apparently intended as a film vehicle for the boy from the valleys, Tom Jones. Working the stage was, he announced, a kind of therapy. 'When people talk of the money and awards I got for writing *Oliver!* I think they're talking about another bloke. In those days I was Flash Harry.' It helped that Joan Littlewood was standing by him, telling anyone prepared to listen that Lionel was a marvellous man who had managed to bury his pride and retrace his steps. It also helped that, at least according to Bart, the world was standing by him: 'hundreds' of letters were tumbling through the door with offers from total strangers – 'just ordinary folk' – promising him a permanent roof over his humble head. Even 'the hob nobs' were moved, apparently, to lay open their summer houses in the Bahamas[3] and Monte Carlo. The dustman offered Bart a sub one morning, and the London cabbies, Gawd bless 'em, were ferrying the pauper across town without so much as a fare being paid – 'on my oath'. It was enough to make a man turn to sentiment, and Bart came up with the saccharine in spoonfuls for the *Daily Mirror*. 'Bart, the man whose music enraptured the world, shook his head wonderingly. "There is still a whole lot of love in this world," he said.'

Not enough, alas, to save him from the courts a second time that year. The following notice appeared on 16 November 1972:

THE COMPANIES ACT 1948. In the Matter of LIONEL BART Limited, Nature of business: Producers & Exhibitors of artistic, dramatic & musical works.

WINDING-UP ORDER MADE 9th October, 1972

DATE and PLACE of 1st MEETINGS:

CREDITORS 28th November 1972 at Room 401 4th Floor, Inveresk House, 346 Strand, London, W.C.2, at 11.30 o'clock

CONTRIBUTORIES on the same day and at the same place at 12.0 o'clock

R. B. HOWARD Official Receiver and Provisional Liquidator

Lionel Bart Limited, whose registered office was at Regent Arcade House, Regent Street, London, had been compulsorily wound up in a ten-second hearing in the High Court on 9 October. And curiously, it was the top people's department store Harrods which had brought this to pass, in pursuit of an unpaid bill for £318. Mr John Bradburn, for the petitioners, told Mr Justice Templeman that they were judgment creditors, and that no other creditors had given notice supporting or opposing the petition. The company was not represented. Three days later everyone's favourite 'bloke' was back there once again, forced to make an apology at the London Bankruptcy Court, where he stated that complicated transactions between himself and limited companies were holding up the production of accounts required in his personal bankruptcy proceedings. These would explain why he had a deficiency of £63,150. While this public examination was adjourned until 25 January, back came Bart on 8 November for the hearing at the High Court between his company Oliver Promotions and the makers of the film of *Oliver!* In desperation, Bart's company was claiming that it was entitled to about £47,000 arising out of agreements that it should receive 6.25 per cent of 'levy monies' paid by the British Film Fund Agency – estimated in the region of £750,000. At issue was whether the levy monies formed part of the gross receipts. The judge ruled against Bart's claim.

As a result of this ruling, Lionel Bart Limited's creditors were told at a meeting on 28 November that the upright piano on which he composed all his songs, together with its stool and some carpeting, were the company's only known assets. The headlines crowed. The exact financial position was hardly clear: apart from Harrods' claim for £318, the Inland Revenue was owed £3,621, although the last accounts (filed over two years earlier, in April 1970) showed that other companies in the Bart group may have been owed £54,000 by Lionel Bart Limited.

Formed in 1957, the company had an issued capital of £1,000, and operated from Bart's flat in Reece Mews. He received between £3,000 and £6,000 a year director's salary for the ten years to 1970. His mother, also a director until her death in 1970, received £3,000 to £5,000. In 1971 Bart resigned as director but continued with company affairs. In the years up to its closure the company's income had varied from a peak of £91,000 in 1966 to £29,000 in 1969 – a swing explained by the assignment of part of Bart's income to another company, when losses were suffered on *Twang!!* after 1965.

Following the creditors' meeting, Bart put on the bravest of faces to match the bravura outfit he was wearing: a huge-brimmed hat and black velvet coat. His own verdict on the catastrophic downfall which seemed never-ending? 'You cannot get sentimental about objects. The piano is an old upright I bought on the never-never back in 1957 when I was beginning to earn a bob or two. I must have written a dozen songs and a thousand shows on it. Even the Beatles and the Rolling Stones have written some of their hits on that old upright.'

Within the fortnight, he was getting understandably maudlin about the full circle his wheel of fortune had just turned. 'My mother,' he told the *Sunday Express* in full tearjerk mode, 'was forty-nine[4] when I was born, by which time she had very little strength left to give me the love and affection I craved. Not only was I deprived of love, I had no money either. So, you can imagine, when I hit it really big with *Oliver!* the novelty of being wealthy was more than I could cope with. Trouble is, money doesn't automatically bring love, does it? And I needed love. So I thought I could buy it. I had this desperate *need* to be loved, you see. And people I considered my friends could get the world out of me. Money was no object. I used to think that giving someone an expensive gift was a foolproof way of buying their admiration. Today, of course, by some irony, the whole thing is reversed. I'm so broke, it is *they* who are giving *me* the gifts. The worst thing about being bankrupt – for me – is that I can no longer afford my secretary or the man who used to take down my music for me – because, as you know, I can't write music myself. The house in Fulham and the castle in Morocco I don't miss at all. But those two people were my life.'

How many times has the pop world issued the same sentiments, whether from Lionel one day or Bros the next? With Bart, it was not entirely the fault of the drink or the drugs. If he was culpable of greed, he was almost equally recklessly generous. If he was arguing his innocence out of stupidity, there was as much cupidity in his network of companies and investments. His world had begun to unravel at least seven years earlier when *Twang!!* dived, but now there was no chance of picking up the loose threads and stitching them back into a seamless garment. Lionel was no longer the sun around which lesser planets revolved. He was not even part of the galaxy. It was no longer a universe of white suede boots and gold lamé suits – unless you were going on stage at the Talk of the Town.

As the music world ushered in glam rock, with the likes of Elton and Bowie camping their way up the charts, Bart was still dining off the success of a show which opened in 1960. His biggest disaster was still warm in its grave, rotting under a heap of yesterday's reputations. The world spun on without stopping to let Bart off. Forced to cling on, he was also forced to watch everything and everyone fly off around him.

In print, Bart was now consistently labelled 'the bankrupt songwriter' which, though referring to his finances, served as well for his creative capital. While Freddie Starr was headlining *Who Do You Do?* on London Weekend Television and with Alan Ayckbourn at the Comedy Theatre with *Time & Time Again*, the best Bart could manage in October 1972 was a shared credit with Frank Norman and Alan Klein in another Joan Littlewood production for Stratford East, called *Costa Packet* – 'a candy-floss entertainment' starring the veteran Avis Bunnage, on the subject of package holiday tours. Among its many faults, according to the *Guardian*, was that, in spite of 'a handful of jolly songs', the drama 'suffers from an outdated attitude...the show seems sociologically dubious and intellectually muddled', and its Donald McGill seaside postcard view of life was quite out of kilter. With this forgettable trifle Joan Littlewood bowed out of the theatre in this country to enter retirement in France. It also marked the last work Lionel Bart was to create for the stage for the next fifteen years.

It was to be only fifteen weeks, however, before Bart made a return appearance in the London Bankruptcy Court, pleading that he never fully understood his financial affairs, and that he signed anything his advisers placed before him. This time, royalties earned by Bart and held by the Performing Right Society were being claimed by Hemdale Group, the film, entertainment and investment company formed by the actor David Hemmings and John Daley. Agreeing that he now had deficiencies of £86,736, Bart's best line of defence was: 'I am not very good at figures'. Once more, the blame was laid on *Twang!!* and losses from other works which had not been produced, together with bad advice, entering into financial guarantees, losses on the sale of the house and living beyond his income. There was a robust exchange between Bart and Mr Royston Howard, the Official Receiver:

MR BART: I have been spending, I have been spending on my work. I have spent very little on myself.

MR HOWARD: Am I right that throughout your career you never really appreciated the state of your financial affairs?

MR BART: Except rather loosely. I was told I was earning a great deal of money, and I let people get on with taking care of it. I signed whatever I was asked to sign.

He continued by explaining that he did not know about the winding up of Lionel Bart Ltd, the company he formed in 1957, until reading the newspapers in the previous October. Asked by Mr Howard if he would be surprised to learn that none of his income tax had been paid on assessment since 1966, Bart replied: 'Nothing would surprise me.' Mr Howard then pointed out that only three days before the bankruptcy petition filed by Bart against himself, the composer had run up a hotel bill of £2,369 in Jamaica. Bart replied: 'I didn't really know I was going to put in the petition until the last moment. I didn't know how bad things really were until the last few days. I went to Jamaica to work. I had stayed there in the past without paying, and I did not make the arrangements myself this time.' He now had a breathing space, as the hearing was adjourned until 12 April 1973.

In the course of the hearing Bart had admitted that by the end of 1969 he realized that he too was going out with the sixties, that the affairs of the companies he had formed were getting out of hand, and that companies to which he owed money would be taking any royalties from successful shows like *Oliver!* for years ahead. Just two years earlier, on the wall of his flat was a chart showing his latest earnings from royalties over a three-month period. They totalled around £20,000. Not bad for a man on the breadline; for a man who had sold the music publishing rights of *Oliver!* to Max Bygraves and Jock Jacobson for £1,000.[5] They eventually resold them for around a million dollars.

Where had Bart's money gone? He was sanguine about it, almost nonchalant, when he told the *Mirror* columnist Jack Bentley: 'I did some potty things in business. At one time I reckon I was paying out about eighty per cent of my earnings to agents and various people I hired.' In the next breath, he was wondering whether to fork out the £3,000 for overhauling his £8,000 Bentley Continental, exactly which Mediterranean resort to flee to in order to escape a muggy March in town, and whether it was time for a third port and brandy. In showbusiness, being broke is a purely relative term. To Bart, it was a rarefied state of mind with which, like reality, he was not then able to come firmly to grips. He was still living in the future, and boasted to Jack Bentley: 'Don't think I've been wasting my time over the last five years. I've got over 400 songs ready to place. Then, there's my film *Punch and Judy* waiting for Trevor Howard and Diana Dors to become available. My musical *Gulliver's Travels* will be produced in Los Angeles in August. My film musical *Ruggles of Red Gap* is due for production, and so is *Quasimodo*, my opera based on *The Hunchback of Notre Dame*. But first things first...and that's an LP I'm making at the moment which is a Negro gospel version of Bernard Shaw's *St Joan*.' What was once merely a chorus was now a constant refrain.

Bart was still whirling round the theatrical world of Shaftesbury Avenue, oblivious to its reluctance to work with a drunk and a box office risk. He was in trouble, he *was* trouble – and he was expensive trouble. It was, arguably, an awesome achievement to go bankrupt within ten years of writing one of the longest-running musicals in the history of the genre. And the composer was showing signs (to anybody who cared to look) of not being able to believe that his golden touch had deserted him – along with so many of his fairweather friends. He failed to hear the boos from the audiences. He refused to accept the unseemly exits of backers, producers and directors. He convinced himself, but nobody else, that every turkey was a fecund golden goose. With the pomp and dependable regularity of Court Circulars, he was not to be silenced from making grandiose pronouncements about his embryonic projects.

CHAPTER NINE

WHERE IS LOVE?

O ne weekend in April 1973 Lionel was staying with friends near
Reading. On the Sunday he found himself in the most unlikely
role – refereeing a knockabout football match between the staff of a
country club and a firm from Pangbourne. After the game he was given
a lift, along with two others, in a Bedford van driven by Graham Chapman.
As the vehicle turned into Oxford Road, Reading, it overturned, injur-
ing all the passengers. Bart and the others found themselves in Reading's
Battle Hospital. While the two back-seat travellers had concussion, Bart
also had multiple injuries. A week later he had recovered sufficiently to
be moved to St Stephen's, opposite his old home and just down the
Fulham Road from his Reece Mews flat. Five broken ribs, a broken
shoulder and a smashed collar-bone gave him excruciating pain, but
couldn't stop him entertaining London's glitterati at his sickbed.
Grouped around the tiny room on one evening were David Bowie,
Donovan, Suzanna Leigh, Ringo Starr and Liza Minnelli, who a few
weeks earlier had won an Oscar for *Cabaret*. When he was finally discharged, after about three weeks, he embarked on a round of house-
guesting, staying first with Donovan, then Pete Townshend, next with

Keith Moon, and after that with Joan Littlewood, with whom he had rekindled the warmth of their friendship at the twentieth anniversary knees-up of Theatre Workshop.

Beneath the surface, things were most certainly not what they used to be. A fortnight before the accident Lionel was forced to apologize at the London Bankruptcy Court for having gone to Spain without making sure he had permission to leave the country. Apparently, he had applied for leave to go abroad, but left for Marbella the day before his application was heard. Despite current debts of £89,310 and assets of just £2,574, he had already been abroad three times since his bankruptcy petition, and assumed he had some kind of 'blanket clearance' to clear off at will. The Marbella trip was supposed to be a three-week working holiday in his manager's seaside villa. It was beginning to anguish the creator of *Oliver!* that the show was now in production around the world – Los Angeles had just opened for a six-month run – while he himself was seeing hardly a penny of the receipts. In a tale of woe told to Ray Connolly, Bart was sounding increasingly pained about the entire turn of his life. Being a bankrupt meant spending needless and tedious hours at the Bankruptcy Court signing papers and waiting in rooms 'where the ash trays are type-writer ribbon tins – lest anybody should make off with more valuable objects'. It also meant he found himself submerged in a wash of pity. Friends would pay for restaurants, taxi drivers belied the meanness of their profession and refused his fare, while even the dustmen waived any 'Christmas-box' with no intention of scattering some refuse around his porch. Bart was not finding it easy to be a bigger taker than a giver. By his reckoning, he had run through $35 million – with a little help from his friends and enemies. Having been told he was earning £2 to £16 a minute, he felt it was reasonable to expect to be able to spend half of it, little realizing that taxation wanted, at that time, around 86 per cent of it. He would jet off to the sun, in whichever part of the world it happened to be shining. He lavished presents on his forty-five god-children[1] and thirty-five nieces and nephews, sending them all something on his own birthday, because he found it unreasonable to keep track of theirs.

One friend who had kept an eye on Lionel was no longer alive to do so. Sir Noël Coward had died on 26 March 1973 in his adopted home

Jamaica. Bart had loved him dearly, and on top of his piano still kept the photograph of the two of them together. In 1962, Noël had helped Bart through his first bout of being boracic, by inviting the young protégé to Switzerland and lending him a large amount of money, which Lionel to his credit repaid within a couple of months. Coward had himself known the same reckless, feckless hardships of showbusiness fortune, where the temptation is for more show, less business. Within hours of Coward's death the speculation and rumours were festering about his lifelong undisclosed sexuality. The change in the law, allowing homosexual acts between two consenting males over twenty-one in private, had only been passed six years earlier in Britain, and prejudices would take another decade to wear down to the point where prominent names in the entertainment world would begin to acknowledge their lifestyles as 'gay'.

Bart has only once publicly accepted his love for men. In the *Daily Mirror* on 6 February 1971 he was caught in a rare, unguarded moment. 'I suppose I'm a Communist, homosexual junkie,'[2] before quickly recovering to deny at least one of his pleasures: 'No, I'm not hooked on drugs. I've gone all through that scene and it isn't worth it when you lose reality.' Connolly, two years later, was closer than any other interviewer in getting him to nail some colours to the mast when he asked why Bart remained unmarried.

'I'm married to *dozens* of people. I'm not married to a lady and I haven't got any children – but I loved one lady who died.[3] I'm a gypsy, mate. I'm also an Arab – you know what I mean? You must know what I mean. I lived in Morocco for three-and-a-half years. To me sex and love are two separate things. And gender is also a separate thing. There's a certain love for a man, a certain love for a boy, a certain love for a woman and a certain love for a girl. And there's not many English ladies who can carry that. A lot pretend to, but there's not many who can.'

Connolly then asks outright if Bart is saying that he is bisexual. After all, David Bowie was only one among dozens of pop stars who were tripping over each other to declare their pansexual desires in this Age of Aquarius. Was Lionel about to join their ranks?

139

'I'm *trisexual*. I don't know...whatever! I'm spontaneous. If I find myself doing any old tricks in bed, or somebody else doing theirs, then it's instant drooperama.'

This was as far as the public would ever be allowed into Bart's bedroom secrets. Today Bart is hardly any more outspoken about his sexuality than he was twenty years ago. In private, however, he will regale any willing audience with tales of Nureyev and one of our leading cinema actors, or with outrageous remarks about, most famously, James Dean. According to Bart's hazy apocryphal anecdote, it was during his first visit to Hollywood that he encountered a pimply, bespectacled Dean at the roadside, hitching a lift. The two 'shacked up together' for a couple of weeks before Dean headed off to New York to practise his other arts in *The Amoralist*. This has always been a behavioural pattern for the wiser, older brother figure, and he coyly confesses to his Diaghilev role by saying that he gets his 'jollies' from new talents...'and from grooving with them. It's like making love. I don't get my jollies unless I'm giving somebody else the same thing.'

His reserve is, perhaps, a lingering habit of a pre-Wolfenden circumspection. One can even glimpse, in *Maggie May*, an admittedly glancing though unnecessary anti-gay remark between the hero Casey and his pal Cogger, who is suspected of unnatural affections for Casey thanks to his sulky attempts to prevent his mate from mating. And Casey himself is the butt of working-class mockery among fellow dockers, who taunt: 'Don't turn your back on him...he's been in the Navy, whoops.' Necessary period authenticity? Perhaps.

Bart's sexuality certainly does not feature in the seventies show that attempted to portray his life on stage. *Lionel* followed in the wake of the massive, and unanticipated, success of *Side by Side by Sondheim*, devised by David Kernan for the Mermaid Theatre in May 1976. Not unlike its subject, however, *Lionel* was not content to be a cabaret evening in which to rediscover some classic show tunes. *Lionel* was a full-scale musical biography which struggled for a few weeks at the New London Theatre in 1977. The producer was David Shaw,[4] and the book was written by his friend, Allan Warren,[5] who was also to have directed the show, but suffered a nervous breakdown before rehearsals, which led to the choreographer Gillian Gregory taking over. John Wells, a colleague of Bart's in Theatre Workshop days, is credited with the revised book. In the cast were fellow Theatre Workshop veteran Avis Bunnage, Adrienne Posta, chanteuse Marion Montgomery, Clarke Peters and (because the idea of the show was that Lionel was a perpetual child, always exploited by the grown-ups) the thirteen-year-old Todd Carty.⁶ An unknown Andrew Logan is thanked in the programme for Occasional Inspiration, which may or may not have led to him being commissioned to make one of his trademark broken-piece mirrors in spectacular dimensions: 16 feet tall and 20 feet wide. The stage manager was Brian Kirk, who still retains a clear picture of events. 'Lionel was in the middle of his dark days then, he was a bit dangerous to have around, and he was eventually barred from the theatre. He was allowed to attend the Dress Rehearsal, however, and I remember him turning up at the stage-door with a teddy bear, which he then had sitting next to him in the stalls throughout. The show itself was fated from the outset. Allan's book was terrible, and the production was cumbersome – we had to winch everything for miles. I've never worked so many all-night sessions as I did on that show. The cast were under no illusions, they were busy organizing their auditions almost on the first day of rehearsal. But the first-night party, held on David Shaw's vast roof-terrace in Belgravia, was the most star-studded I've ever attended: Mick Jagger was there, Rod Stewart was there, but there was no sign of Lionel. The notices, needless to say, were terrible, and the show limped on for five weeks. I reckon that it cost a quarter of a million pounds in 1977...equivalent to two million today.' Among those notices, *The Times* admits, 'What they hoped to do is hard to tell'. Bernard Levin, writing in the *Sunday Times*, dismisses it as a 'desperately unimaginative and ugly production, together with somewhat orthopaedic choreography'.

Lionel himself, when anyone could be persuaded to listen, was still talking ardently – and a little too often – of the work that was gushing from him at a rate to shame the seven dwarves. He was still, year on year, 'just completing' his mammoth production of *The Hunchback of Notre Dame* – a pipe-dream which brought him sharply in contact with sooty reality, when he met the book-writer Mark Bramble. Bramble is an American who resides either in New York or London, having hatched for himself two golden eggs: he wrote or co-wrote the books of *Barnum* and *42nd Street*, among others. Bart's agent at the time was the extremely protective Patricia Macnaughton, and it was she who contacted Bramble (also her client), with a view to him taking a look at *Blitz!* prior to a revival, pencilled with the Royal Shakespeare Company. The all-American sophisticate took the material with him on a holiday to Italy with the set designer Robin Don, but found it 'too foreign. Not being Jewish or Cockney, and not having lived through the Blitz, I just felt I had to reject the offer.' Macnaughton, however, knew she needed a turbine to propel Lionel out of his creative inertia, and tried to tempt Bramble with a second project, this time not a revival but the unfinished *Quasimodo*. He was given four cassettes, each containing a different version of the show's demo songs, and was invited to listen to the tapes before an arranged lunch with Lionel. Well before the meeting this material too was returned to the agent, with another apology: 'This is really not for me.' Mark Bramble had not read Hugo's *Notre Dame de Paris* and, though he had seen William Dieterle's movie, he found it impossible to determine from the demo tapes whether or not the score was sound, despite recalling 'a couple of very strong ballads.'

Finally Patricia Macnaughton asked whether, in the climate of Bart making a modest comeback, Bramble might not cast his eye over some of Lionel's old shows as well as those yet to be completed. Bramble agreed, and the lunch took place at Jake's Restaurant on London's Fulham Road. Bramble recalls that 'Lionel was delightful, absolutely delightful and very entertaining...though he was wearing far too much make-up, that old Hollywood pancake make-up that you apply with a sponge. Over lunch we discussed a number of ideas and projects, including a musical based on the comic-strip character *Dick Tracy*, though within minutes of returning to her office, Patricia had discovered that Warren Beatty owned the rights.' It was clear that Lionel passionately wanted to complete *Quasimodo*, and told Bramble proudly that it had been written over the course of one weekend while stoned out of his mind, and that he was thrilled when Noël Coward said, on hearing it: 'It's brilliant, but it doesn't make a bit of sense to me, boy.'

In the summer of '84 Bramble made his annual pilgrimage to Fire Island, where the New York theatre posse gathers for its aestival R & R, only to be pursued by Patricia Macnaughton on the telephone, wondering whether he would reconsider a collaboration on the hunchback story. He agreed to the request, and set about taking Hugo's melodrama to the beach each day, becoming immediately attracted to the story of a twenty-year-old Quasimodo and a sixteen-year-old Esmerelda. And that was the story he wanted to tell. Lionel, however, had always contemplated a leading character player in the mould of Zero Mostel – a physical, Laughtonesque actor, but of a certain age. It was only one of many disagreements to emerge over the next eighteen months of their fruitless union. From New York, Bramble spoke to Macnaughton and expressed his keenness to work *The Hunchback* up into the book for a musical, but insisted on it being clear from the beginning that if he and Lionel were unable to work together satisfactorily, he fully intended to continue alone, and reserved the right to create a stage musical based on Victor Hugo's original work. It was to be a useful insurance policy, in the event.

By the time Mark Bramble returned to the elegant Covent Garden home that the proceeds of *Barnum* and *42nd Street* had enabled him to buy, Lionel, the now penniless creator of the world's longest-running musical, was in a high state of excitement. Victor Spinetti[7] had joined him as collaborator, without Bramble's knowledge, and they had begun drafting the book of *Quasimodo*. There was a new script, of sorts, and a sheaf of new songs had been outlined within the dramatic structure, which Bart was now proposing to embark on. The ill-assorted three-some continued to work 'together' as best they could, though each recognized from their first joint meeting that there was just no chemistry in the project. According to Bramble, his two fellow authors would spend much of their time together talking about themselves and their shared theatrical reminiscences of Stratford East, rather than about the show they had agreed to complete. And yet the industrious Victor came up with scene after scene of scripted book.

In late August Mark Bramble accompanied a colleague to the Edinburgh Festival, where one of the many fringe shows they took in was a National Youth Theatre production, transferred from London, of *Murder in the Cathedral*. The friend explained to the American what the NYT's status was: a charitable company founded to enable untrained actors under the age of twenty-three to 'have a go' during a summer season of rehearsals and performances, all professionally directed, designed and staged.

Bramble was impressed with the level of achievement. Indeed, impressed enough to request a meeting with the company's director Ed Wilson, and to visit the NYT's expansive rehearsal space in north London. It seemed an ideal venue and an adventurous enough company to workshop the putative blockbuster. The response from Wilson and his team was positive, and Bart and Bramble were invited to a forthcoming rehearsal, at which Bramble (who at this stage was also to have directed *Quasimodo*) could consider the available company and begin thinking about possible casting. At the chosen rehearsal, the first sparks flew when Lionel objected to Bramble's note-taking, accusing him of undermining the confidence of the company. Lionel was evidently very resistant to any idea of workshopping *his* long-brewed infusion with such raw energies. Bramble, by contrast, was encouraging the experiment as a safe haven in which to look at the work, contemplate its structure, its weaknesses and prepare for its overhaul. And yet, ironically, it was this first encounter which subsequently relaunched Bart's latter-day theatrical moment on the London stage.

They were equally at odds over who should design the eventual masterpiece. Bart, as is now commonly acknowledged, often created a show around a Sean Kenny set. These monstrous structures gave life to the musicals, just as they sapped life from them. Bart had met the ballet designer Peter Docherty, and found in him a charisma as attractive as that which he had lost in Sean. He determined that Docherty was his chosen interpreter for *Quasimodo*. Bramble, who was now also directing transfers and tours of *42nd Street*, remained equally adamant that Docherty's friend and colleague from the opera stage, Robin Don, was the only person with the required vision for a musical on such a scale.

The workshops never happened. The Spinetti–Bart–Bramble axis produced, after a lengthy gestation, just the book of Act One. 'There was never,' explains Bramble, 'a line of lyric, never a note of music. At least, not presented to me. And then, one of Lionel's four sisters became acutely ill, and died quite suddenly. Within a few days, Lionel sent me a telegram with his termination note. I remember the telegram on blue paper, because it was thought by everyone to be quite a rare means of communication in today's world. And that was it really. It had become clear that he didn't really want to do it. And the entire project just drifted away.'

Drifted away from Bart. But not from Bramble, who seized his moment. Having reserved the rights to continue work on a musicalization of Victor Hugo's *Notre Dame de Paris*, he did just that, and set about finding himself a composer. A draft book was completed in October 1986, but because of the distractions of directing an Australian version of *42nd Street* in the summer of '87 for the producer Helen Montagu (who had also nurtured the show to award-winning status at London's Theatre Royal, Drury Lane), it was not until autumn 1987 that Bramble could return to London and start once again the collaborative process: this time with Robert Butler on the book and with Callum Macleod and Paul Leigh on the music. Their eventual progeny was to be work-shopped for just three performances at the new Lilian Baylis studio theatre, within the historic Sadler's Wells. The event was heralded by an announcement in the showbusiness weekly the *Stage*, which Lionel read with irrepressible fury. Mark Bramble recollects the following sequence of events.

'Lionel telephoned on the Thursday morning on which the *Stage* was published. He pleaded with me :" Don't do this to my idea." I replied that my production *was* going forward, and reminded Lionel of my original declaration of reserved rights. Then a letter arrived from Harbottle & Lewis, Lionel's lawyers, in which there was a reference to my having been "privilege to his ideas and material"...which was meaningless, since Victor Hugo's book is in the public domain, it's out of copyright in other words, and anyway there have been dozens of versions of *The Hunchback* story all over the world. More than that, Lionel Bart had had no "ideas or material" – not that he'd presented to me at any rate!

Harbottle & Lewis also requested a copy of my script, and my own solicitor advised me to invite Lionel Bart and Victor Spinetti to the opening at the Lilian Baylis, which I did, and told them that a script would be available at that time, partly because it was still undergoing daily revisions. Four seats were reserved for them on opening night. Victor Spinetti turned up with a friend, but the seats reserved for Lionel remained empty.[8]

'Following that, I heard nothing from Lionel except for one threatening phone call, where he accused me of stealing his idea, and saying that he would seek revenge through the press and that the press would be sympathetic to him...ending up with him screaming, "I'll get you for this." The whole episode was a heartbreak for me. *Oliver!* was the first show I ever saw, and Lionel was a great hero of mine. Maybe there's the moral – never put your faith in old heroes.'

At the root of Lionel's possessive aggression over *Quasimodo*, there lay perhaps a deeper anxiety: arguably, the self-realization that he would never – that nobody *could* ever – repeat the breathtaking success of *Oliver!* in the musical theatre. He was constantly to attempt to regenerate the formula of taking a schoolboy classic like *The Hunchback* or *Gulliver*, smoothing its edges, adding a love interest, a chorus line and an exclamation mark or two, and storming the West End. Reality was not something Lionel was adapting to very easily – or very successfully. In 1972 he wrote music (incorporating sounds from a south London scrapyard, a Thames-side rubbish dump and a multi-racial school) and lyrics for Peter Sellers to sing in the film *The Optimists of Nine Elms*. It's a sentimental fantasy story centred on Sellers as a vaudevillian scraping pennies as a busker with his faithful mongrel at his side and two Bisto-kids on his coat-tails. Originally he was to have been a Cockney, which landed like manna in Bart's lap. But two days before shooting, the script was altered to make him North Country, leaving Bart to attempt a pastiche George Formby on the score. In the film, the music is credited to George Martin, protector and producer of the Beatles.

This was almost the only creative work of any substance that the declining talent completed during the next two decades. The bluster went on about *Quasimodo*, as it was now being called, and how it was now going to be a double album with Richie Havens, to be followed by a film with Marlon Brando. *Gulliver's Travels* was slated for Christmas '73 at the Mermaid...there was talk of Bernard Miles's perennial treat *Treasure Island* transferring to the big screen with Keith Moon, Viv (Bonzo Dog) Stanshall and Harry Nilsson...there were the three movies and four stage shows 'being offered every week', which included a film project with the equally rock-bottom Mae West, a musical based on *The Water Babies*, and a production of Brendan Behan's *Borstal Boy*. All that commissioning managements ever saw of their longed-for hits was the occasional press report on the progress Lionel claimed to be making – all the while evaporating his advances with decreasing amounts of soda water added. His excuses? 'It's not that I haven't got the discipline, it's just that I don't like working alone any more. It's a bit like jerking off. I think it takes two people to make a bit of magic – at least two people. But when the songs are needed they come right off the top.' Though that is just what they did not do – certainly not to order. Every ounce of the optimism that led him to believe he might one day, for example, build a theatre-world in Australia where people would live and share their children and food while making beautiful drama, was tempered by a black dog of despair that told him he could have been happy as plain old Lionel Begleiter without an expensive nose-job. While his life-force was supplied by liquid, his life had no liquidity. He was living on £65 a week, which lasted about a day. His appeal for a bigger slice of the profits from the screen version of *Oliver!* failed in May 1974, with a ruling that his company Oliver Productions Limited was not entitled to any percentage of levy-monies from the film.

Lionel was still trying to believe that it would all come right, that the good times would return and that, when they did, they would go on for ever. He tried surrounding himself with lawyers, managers, accountants, agents and advisers, all of whom lost patience with the ageing, awkward alcoholic that Bart had become. If he now refers to the seventies and eighties as his Rip van Winkle years, it is not just that he is unable to recall the events, the faces or the places that occupied his brief attention span, but that to do so would bring back the haunting shame and self-loathing of those days. He would turn up at the Savoy Hotel bar with a three-day beard, and without the regulation jacket and tie, simply to test the theory that they would capitulate to this impropriety for no other reason than that he was Lionel Bart, capital L capital B. He was often too drunk even to enjoy their unctuous reaction, but was determined, out of spite, to hit rock-bottom in order to turn his face up to the leering crowds and slur: 'Look, there's nothing left for you to envy. Just a clown on his backside.'

As he now admits, he woke up one day to realize that he had become his own audience. Nobody else was looking. No one was interested in a former songwriter who couldn't stop shaking long enough to hold a pen. His drying-out sessions lasted as long as one of Liz Taylor's diets and, like the former movie queen, he continued to allow himself to be fêted for his once glittering achievements, while turning into a professional clinic-hopper. Few of his former 'friends' were capable of helping – let alone willing to get involved. Arguably, Lionel himself should take some blame for never allowing any single person to come close enough to form a lasting emotional bond. Arguably, too, this was because Lionel considered himself unlovable.

Was this humbling period of self-loathing born of his belief that he would never be the simple, unaffected 'mensch' his father had wanted? How much more of himself would Bart need to reject before he could tolerate or banish the rejection that his father had unwittingly inflicted on the sensitive son? The psychologist Dr Anthony Storr[9] attempts to locate:

> the need for creative people to rebel against the past. This rebellion is often more impersonal than personal. That is, it is against ideas, techniques and points of view rather than against people...the creative person may be a revolutionary on the intellectual plane, but remain emotionally tied to his parents. In this way his identity as a thinker or creator may be established, whilst his identity as a person may not.... More ordinary people rebel directly and personally against their parents, especially in adolescence, and this is an important step in achieving a sense of identity. This sense is later reinforced both by acquiring a role in life in terms of work, and also by an increasing definition of

individuality through the formation of new relationships outside the family, especially with the opposite sex.

It may be simplistic to draw any analogy of cause-and-effect between an artist's background and that necessary sand which drives the oyster to close its shell and spend its life creating one matchless pearl for the world to admire. But, according to Storr, apart from gaining the desired self-esteem by producing a work which wins recognition, the creative artist:

> can allow to emerge in his work the aggressive feelings which he finds such difficulty in expressing in real, day-to-day encounters with other people. Getting one's own back on parents is, of course, a favourite pastime.... Many people of this temperament, during the course of childhood and adolescence, give up hope of being loved for themselves, especially since they habitually conceal their real natures. But the hope raises itself again when they start to create; and so they become intensely sensitive about what they produce, more sensitive than they are about their own defended personalities in ordinary social life.

Who knows whether, without that bruising that may even now not have fully healed, Lionel Begleiter would have become the Bart who gave us *Oliver!* or 'Living Doll'.

Lionel himself believes he was driven to the limits of excess by the same impulses that drove him to the limits of success – the impulse to be rich and to escape his East End Jewishness. And yet, how he could have created musicals like *Blitz!* or *Fings* without that background is inconceivable. So, at once the source of his achievements and the curse of his later years, his origins could hardly be held responsible for the routine he had imposed on himself: to kick open the day with a bottle of vodka, and finish at least two more by the end of it. As he has always admitted, he never actually enjoyed the taste of alcohol, having hated it since being given sips of cherry brandy as a child by his aunts. But like any alcoholic, Bart learned that it was the quickest route to oblivion. And if, like other alcoholics, Bart was hoping that that oblivion would also enable him to drown any lingering sorrows, what might those sorrows be, other than increasing self-loathing?

Throughout his life, there had never been (for any significant period) a stabilizing emotional anchor, no Peter Pears to his Benjamin Britten. His greatest personal loss had come in 1973. Bart's lifelong friend, drinking partner and collaborator Sean Kenny died, of what Bart calls 'a brain explosion'. And though Sean had never been a real object of physical love, he returned a love that contained – ironically in the circumstances in which he predeceased Bart – a concern that Bart would seriously damage his health through his lifestyle.

Leslie Bricusse,[10] who had shared a holiday villa with Bart in Portofino in the late sixties, still finds it difficult to understand how things could go so wrong. 'We used to see a great deal of Lionel, either at Peter Noble's parties, or at Alma Cogan's place in Stafford Court, off Kensington High Street.[11] And then we met again in New York in 1962, because *Oliver!* opened there the same season as *Stop the World, I Want to Get Off.* In fact, at some point or other, I remember we formed the LB Club, for all those who shared our initials...so our patron was Beethoven, and the members included Lionel Blair, Lauren Bacall and so on. I got fairly concerned about Lionel between about November 1959 and July 1960 when he had three shows on, and then when *Oliver!* opened on Broadway, he suddenly became very aware of the money he was earning, and just started to squander it. He was at all the right places, he absolutely loved being the success he was, and being at the centre of everything...Lionel, with his jargon, his patter, he was a natural star for the press. In fact, he was the only person I know who had a *real* friendship with Judy Garland, they adored each other. And whoever advised him to give up his publishing to United Artists should never have been allowed to, because I remember in 1967 or '68 he played *Quasimodo* for my wife Yvie and myself, and I thought it would be a sure success. It just seems that it's possible to frighten yourself into a form of non-creativity, and Lionel may have paralysed himself in terms of "How do I restart?" – just wondering what to do for an encore...once you have reached the summit, nobody can keep up there all the time.' When Bart, uncontrollably affected by alcohol and other substances, gave great offence to Yvie at a party in Gstaad, Bricusse decided it was time to draw a line under their twenty years of friendship.

By 1976, Lionel was somehow managing to keep at least one project on the boil, though it was surely one of the least likely musical projects after *Springtime for Hitler*. Bart had been invited to Israel to meet Golda Meir, with a view to writing a stage show based on her life story, in collaboration with Roger Cook – doubtless with a view to asking lifelong Meir fan Barbra Streisand to take the title role. Bart and Meir met in the security fortress of the Knesset, where he claims to have composed a song on the spot, which led to the prime minister announcing: 'You got the job, but lay off the romance.' A reference, Bart assumed, to wanting to protect the feelings of her husband. From 1977 to 1984 the project simply gathered dust on a shelf, then the film company Cannon began to show an interest, as they did in so many offbeat ideas which helped hasten their financial ruin.

The 'Golda Story' was, in fact, the first project on which Lionel Bart and Mark Bramble jointly exercised their talents, when it was clear Warren Beatty wanted to run with *Dick Tracy*. Bramble, who had been given what there was of the show's material by Patricia Macnaughton, was by now very friendly with Georgia Brown, who was playing Dorothy Brock in his London production of *42nd Street*. Brown, of course, went back all the way to *Oliver!*, and was Bart's own initial choice for the eponymous Israeli political legend. Bramble found the outline script unreadable: it lacked a point of view, and in his opinion could hardly be called the work of a dramatist. There was, though, a demo tape containing some 'not bad songs' and an overall score that had promise. Again, the territory was unfamiliar, if not entirely alien, to the Ivy League American. But he could envisage Miss Brown playing Mrs Meir, and was as attracted to the concept as Georgia herself.

Bramble began a four-month spell of research on his unlikely subject matter, and devised a concept for the musical, to be set in Golda Meir's kitchen, from which the Jewish matriarch would run the country, fuelled by freshly brewed coffee and long-stewed chicken soup. The time frame was the Yom Kippur war, when she had to make the crucial diplomatic decision whether to send Israel's troops to battle against an invading Egyptian army. She cooked and brewed through the night and, throughout the dark hours, she telephoned the people who mattered to her. By dawn, she had determined that her people would fight, and gave her command to go ahead. This kitchen cabinet gave a framework for telling Golda Meir's remarkable life story, much as *Funny Girl*[12] used the conceit of the actress in her dressing-room on the day her husband is released from prison.

Bramble's treatment ran to two or three pages, and was a conspicuous improvement on the William Gibson[13] play for Anne Bancroft, which tried to cover chronologically far too much material. Bart and Patricia Macnaughton were invited to Bramble's Covent Garden apartment, at that time located at the top of a converted warehouse in Lichfield Street. Still gasping for air when he finally reached the top of the stairs, Lionel was quick with his response. Before even looking at the material he delivered a surprising pronouncement: 'I can't do this show. I can't get behind its politics any more.'

Not unlike his creative progress, Bart's financial ruin had reached its own turning point. The debts which originally bankrupted him were in the region of £153,000. Following subsequent research, the true figure was discovered to be nearer £73,000 – less than half. Thus it was that at Lionel's bankruptcy discharge in 1976 the registrar issued a severe reprimand to the songwriter's former financial advisers. From this moment on, for almost an entire decade, there is little record of Bart's public activities – no newspaper cuttings, no photographs, no personal appearances. He was assumed by many to have died of acute liver poisoning, or at best to have some seedy existence as a down-and-out in some corner of America. A nadir was ultimately reached by 1980. Bart finally sent out an SOS to his East End friend from National Service days in the RAF, John Gorman. John first took Lionel into his care and into his home, where he helped him convalesce. Afterwards, he began to disentangle Bart's notoriously labyrinthine financial mess, becoming his former business partner's new business manager, a co-signatory to all Lionel's cheques, in an effort to protect an unwitting drunk from any further catastrophic moves. According to Gorman, 'Lionel was taken to the cleaners. I think the people who were advising him thought, "He doesn't know what's going on, he doesn't seem to care and he ain't gonna survive it anyway. In a few years he'll be dead." But maybe he was so drunk at the end, you couldn't do anything with him, because he wouldn't listen.'

CHAPTER TEN

BE BACK SOON

'I used to be a flash git who had everything, saw everything and got a kick out of being a celebrity. Now I've got nothing except for one thing that counts – and that's a sense of reality. From now on I want to be me. Just a working fella who is trying to earn a crust. This time I'm not going to be duped out of a penny. That has been the trouble. At one time I reckon I was paying out about eighty per cent of my earnings to agents and various people I hired. I haven't had a business mind.' Having sold his stake in the film of *Oliver!* for £200,000, and after cashing in a quarter of a million stocks and shares, Bart was back at his £5-a-week Reece Mews flat and feeling aggrieved as he sat, cigarette in hand, reviewing the situation. 'I shouldn't have done it. It was like whoring. It just needs *Gulliver's Travels* or *Hunchback* to succeed...and it will happen, I'm sure. Why is it I always have to prove I'm not a flash in the pan? Maybe it's because I'm not an intellectual. I'm just an ordinary bloke who can whistle a song. Now I'm ready to graft again. I'll tell you what I'm going to do this time, I'm going to buy an island in the sun and take over a bunch of kids and we'll live like they do in a kibbutz. We'll grow our own food and do our own things. And maybe we'll make a film and show the world where life is at...'

With each passing year Bart appeared to be regressing into childhood and fantasy, constantly in need of reassurance or attention, devoid of self-confidence, helpless to the point of inertia. As one of his closest friends of the present day expresses it: 'Lionel has made an art form of self-destruction, he seems to take pleasure in destroying what he has created. When he loses his temper, he's like a child stamping its foot, and yet in the next breath he beams and throws his arms around you. He can be a very charming man...there's great kindness as well as a vile temper and a desire to hide himself away. And yet, he's very clear about the part he played in bringing about his own downfall. He accepts that, whatever happened, he created most of it himself.'

Lionel entered his fifties a very unhappy and a very unwell person. In 1978 the three-bottles-a-day composer learned that he had diabetes, and he was ordered by his doctor to abstain from alcohol and follow a strict diet. Yet in June 1980 he was again admitted to hospital for 'a few weeks, for tests...and to get sorted out. I've had a few problems over the drinking.' The backsliding came just as his old collaboratrix Joan Littlewood was planning to revive *Fings*, *Blitz!* and *The Good Soldier Schweik* in a return season at Stratford East, and just a few months after the Christmas revival of *Oliver!* at the Albery.[1] By now, Lionel had given up his South Kensington lifestyle in name as well as in nature, and in spite of talking about his desire to return to the East End to buy into a new riverside development in the former Docklands of Wapping, he was forced to depend on the kindness of strangers,[2] and moved out west to a first- and second-floor flat above a parade of shops in deeply unfashionable, suburban Acton. As if moving straight into harm's way, the shop next door was an off-licence, while the one below Lionel's flat was occupied by a firm of accountants. His lifestyle was, to all appearances, modelled on that of Miss Havisham: unpacked skips of huge press-cutting books blocked the landing, boxes bursting with jumbled, yellowing photos cluttered every spare corner, piles of appointment diaries from forgotten decades were strewn across coffee tables. Day-to-day needs were brought upstairs by his daily help Brenda: Bart seemingly incapable of buying tea, milk or sugar. A close eye was kept on him by his nephew Sammy or by a devoted personal assistant. Apart from necessary

155

supplies of his favourite Guerlain *L'Heure Bleue* perfume (a taste inherited from his sister), possessions were kept to essentials – essentials being
the framed photographs of Lionel with a galaxy of celebrities, the hand-
painted clavichord, a few hundred books and far too many hats. In his
personal appearance something had mellowed: because he was overweight ('by at least two stones') he now favoured a baggy-suited
look...always dressed in black, but still at the cutting edge of affordable
fashion.

By March 1983, after a spell in a drying-out clinic in Wiltshire, he
was back in hospital, this time suffering from pneumonia, which had
opportunistically attacked the remnants of a body he relentlessly
wrecked. However, he suddenly discharged himself to attend a magistrates' court hearing at Thame, Oxfordshire. Bart admitted driving in
the town six months earlier with twice the legally permitted level of
alcohol in his blood, after having been stopped for motoring erratically
at 20–30 m.p.h. His lawyer agreed that her client had 'drunk several
glasses of beer at a country fair', which led the magistrate, after hearing
that Lionel had been convicted for a similar offence in 1975, to ban him
for three years, fining him £100 with £105 costs. That summer he was
back on form, at least in the imagination of his agent Patricia
Macnaughton, who diligently confirmed that Lionel 'is in the country
working towards a new musical. Yes, it could be a sequel to *Mary Poppins*
and yes, David Bowie's name has been mentioned in connection with it.
I can say no more. I think I've said enough.' Of all the strange partnerships Bart may or may not have forged, this would have been no stranger
than his collaboration with Bertrand Russell.

Meanwhile Bart could only look on as Ron Moody returned to the
Aldwych Theatre this time, for another Christmas revival of the show
that should have secured its composer's eternal fortune. On tour the
production had already grossed £500,000, and Bart was invited to
become a 'consultant' to the West End transfer, 'because the money
comes in useful'. And, despite his claim that he tried to be anonymous
these days, it was still his show, and the newspapers still wanted a photograph of him with the latest generation of orphans and urchins. Lionel
would always oblige.

For the next two years life was once again a rollercoaster of grindingly slow uphill climbs (particularly in view of his unpredictable health) and headlong rushes back towards the bigtime. First came the news that Steven Spielberg had asked Lionel to write the score for his film version of Barrie's *Peter Pan*. The pair were reported to have met in June 1984 while Spielberg was in London for the première of *Indiana Jones and the Temple of Doom*. Johnny Speight,[3] creator of Alf Garnett, was working with Bart on a musical for Max Bygraves called *The Wally*. Their fond belief was that Max would jump at the chance to send himself up on stage. Bart was also approached by Adam Faith to conceive a musical version of the popular television series *Budgie*,[4] but pleaded that he was too busy with his own staging of the life of the diminutive painter Toulouse-Lautrec. Not only that: he was also writing an American musical based on a charity project called *Magic Me*, where kids go out and help the elderly. Then, almost without warning, he was headline news again. The punkish, studentish, hippyish, nerdish cast of an anarchic television comedy series called *The Young Ones* decided to send up the all-time Mr Clean hero of the suburban housewife, Cliff Richard. To do this, they released a cover version of his first number one hit 'Living Doll'. Cliff's original recording remained intact, but was overlaid by ribald comments in a manner taken up more recently by the cartoon anti-heroes Beavis and Butthead. To everyone's astonishment, this novelty single returned Bart's 1959 creation to the top of the charts in March 1986. Bathing momentarily in the spotlight, Lionel admitted: 'It's such a buzz to have this hit. All these kids singing and whistling it on the street.' While others involved in the project donated their royalties unequivocally to the Comic Relief Fund, Lionel decided that a little bit of charity should start at home. 'Living Doll' was one of the few publishing rights he still owned, and his percentage of over 700,000 sales gave him an even bigger buzz than the odd delivery boy with a tune to hum. And in April the song's born-again success ensured a rapturous ovation from the members of the songwriters' trade association at their annual lunch. Lionel was awarded a special Ivor Novello for his achievements.

As if his wheel of fortune now revolved biennially, 1988 marked a downward turn. In March the press reported that he had walked out of what was to be his comeback show, *Winnie*, the musical celebration of Winston Churchill starring Robert Hardy (renowned for playing Churchill and the vet Siegfried on television, but who had only once before appeared in a musical) with Virginia McKenna as his darling wife Clementine. The production previewed in Manchester, prior to its run at the Victoria Palace, but Bart, choreographer Molly Molloy and three cast members[5] who left with him denounced the show as 'total and absolute chaos'. In defence of the overall artistic venture, *Winnie's* executive producer felt obliged to make a statement: 'The creation of a new musical is a very painful but not, we hope, destructive, experience. There have been problems with the script. It keeps changing every day, and that, I think, is what upset Bart and the others. Various roles became somewhat reduced, and those actors involved became upset.' *Winnie* took the unremarkable form of a play-within-a-play, set shortly after the end of the war when two troupes of actors decide to stage a tribute to the revered leader. When the wartime epic opened in London[6] music and lyrics were credited as 'Various', and included any number of popular nostalgic favourites like 'Bless 'em All' and 'There'll Always Be an England', with additional songs by Cyril Ornadel and Arnold Sundgaard.

As suddenly again, Bart was in the press for more auspicious reasons. After a spell in the wilderness so long that many had thought him dead, Lionel manages to write a new hit song. It is just fifty-eight seconds long. It has a catchy, simple chorus. It is the outcome of almost a year's work by the creative director of the ad agency Publicis. And it advertises the benefits of the country's second-largest building society. Tim Mellors had started work on the account, and had in mind a scenario like a surreal children's pantomime. 'We'd come up with the copy Abbey Endings, and we had started to cast some kids. One day, I was having lunch with Lionel – we'd met through mutual friends when he emerged from the primordial swamp of his drugs and drinking – and he talked about the Opies[7] and their collection of songs, often with internal rhymes. Then I mentioned *Oliver!* in this connection, and he suddenly said that he wouldn't mind having a go at writing a song for the commercial. It hadn't occurred to me until he suggested it, but the more I thought about it, the more I saw that Lionel's work had a naiveté and a natural charm and a sense of childhood which would fit with our concept. I knew that Spielberg had contacted him about working on *Hook* and that that approach had made Lionel very nervous, but I felt that this advert could provide a way-in for him.

'Nothing happened for a week or two, and as we approached the date of the Abbey National flotation and the start of the television campaign, I would ring up and ask if anything had come up. We eventually met for a picnic in a park in Marylebone. He had got his scribe to take down five tunes, and they were all good...the hardest part was to choose which one to use. They were simple, childlike little tunes. I felt encouraged, but it was another age before the lyrics appeared. To Lionel, it was a major step to be writing again, and so I didn't want to distress him, but it was a real exercise in patience for me. You forgive Lionel characteristics that would drive you mad in anybody else. A word a week was about the rate it was produced, but once he got that first draft under his belt he became very enthusiastic. We had lunch with the director Tony Kaye, and Lionel sang a few songs. The idea then occurred to us that we should centre the ad around Lionel himself, cast as something of a Pied Piper. We held the auditions for the kids after advertising in the papers with the line IF YOU CAN SING – COME ALONG, whereupon a thousand children turned up...though Lionel managed to coax that naturalness out of them. Finally, when it came to filming, we had to mock up Lionel playing the piano, and he was very bad tempered a lot of the time, but he still showed tremendous patience with the kids, who were screaming at him "Mister, don't you know any other songs?" and "Why don't yer take yer 'at off?" The finished commercial, I must say, had an almost magical feeling, and it seemed to touch a chord with the public. We were inundated with responses from people as soon as it went out.'

And, not long after, from record companies. According to Mellors, four expressed an interest in releasing the ad as a full-length single, with EMI finally offering the best deal – and talking about a CD! Lionel had, remarkably and admirably, fought his way back from the abyss of self-destruction, yet Tim Mellors considers that the glory and the sudden, unfamiliar acclaim may have dazzled the man who constantly referred to his recent emergence from the Rip van Winkle years. 'For Lionel, it was a kind of rebirth, and it gave him renewed confidence. When 'Happy Endings'[8] came out, he went on rather too many talk-shows, which actually led to him retreating back into himself. What he needed was a torch: the publicity searchlight he received tended to blind him, and he did what he describes as "an ostrich".'

Refusing to be cowed by press reports that his own former Fun Palace had just been sold for £1.5 million[9] by its latest owner, Bart remained buoyant, and could now boast about his years of achievement. This time, however, the boast was not about any creative process (real or imagined); rather it was a confession, at last, that he had needed and sought help for an addiction that had both paralysed and stigmatized him. 'In the end I got sick and tired of waking up the next day not knowing what I'd done or who I'd insulted. There are many people in showbiz with drink problems, and we help each other. I was helped by a lot of love. The difference between now and the old days is that I'm prepared to accept love and support. This is going to be my last comeback. I've recorded "Happy Endings" and I'm back in the spotlight. But I know how to handle the pressures now, and walk away from something I don't want to do. The song in the advert is my song. I'm determined to have a happy ending.'

In common with most members of the self-help organization Alcoholics Anonymous, Bart attends two or three times a week, choosing from over 500 weekly meetings in London alone: sometimes at the West London group known as 'Stars on Sunday' because of the number of minor celebrities and groupies who attend, less often at the Gold Card meeting, which invites only wealthy or famous members, occasionally at a gays-only gathering. The AA programme for recovering alcoholics who want to remain 'dry' is known as the Twelve Steps, and it can be summed up as an admission of powerlessness over alcohol, a belief in a higher power or in God, a confession of past wrongs to a sponsor or close friend (Lionel himself has sponsored at least eight members), a willingness to change and a commitment to others still suffering the effects of alcohol. The camaraderie within AA is extremely close and, like many others, Bart has forged some of his strongest friendships behind its closed doors.

Bart's dogged effort to rid himself of this demon was now revered and increasingly rewarded. On New Year's Eve 1989 his liver began to haemorrhage, and he was taken into intensive care. He stared death in the face from a hospital bed where he was hardly responding to treatment for a secondary infection of pneumonia. He had by now successfully quit drinking, and immediately gave up smoking and spent two months in a lingering convalescence, part of it with Richard O'Brien[10] and his family in Brighton. Interviewed on 1 August 1990, the morning of his sixtieth birthday, he was by turns modest and vainglorious. 'I'm trying to mark the day with silence. I'm very excited about the future, having to prove myself to producers who thought I'd retired. It's like being the new boy at school. Now I'm working on a revival of *Blitz!*, creating a workshop based on *Quasimodo*, working on a film, and *Omnibus*[11] are following me around with a camera, doing a profile.' The revival of *Blitz!* Lionel was working on was not the one he had hoped for. Neither was it the one originally planned at the beginning of the year. In January Britain's most prestigious theatrical shrine, the Royal Shakespeare Company, led by Terry Hands in his valedictory year, had announced a revival of the wartime epic (which Coward had memorably summarized as 'twice as long and twice as loud as the original') to mark the fiftieth anniversary of the Nazi bombing of London. This landmark production (by a company with a reputation for musical failures like *Carrie*) was also to have been the vehicle for the British theatre debut of Hollywood star Bette Midler or, failing that, Georgia Brown, and was due to open at the Company's London home in the Barbican in September. Throughout the run-up, however, there were rumours about the show's failure to ignite: Bart had been 'revising' the show for over a year, supposedly composing five new numbers, with help on updating the book from the tyro East End dramatist Tony Marchant and director Barry Kyle; the RSC was short of the funds necessary to mount a full-scale revival; and by March it was clear that the RSC was to go dark from November for at least four months in order to reduce its cash deficit. Bart did not take the news too stoically. When an arts reporter[12] telephoned Bart for his opinion before leaking the story on BBC Radio 4, the thwarted composer screamed threats of libel, claiming that any chance of finding a commercial backer to salvage the production for a West End run were now nil thanks to such an irresponsible broadcast. However, the story was repeated in the print media within forty-eight hours, with Hands reportedly saying that the project was 'too risky'.

Lionel proved once more that he was blessed with indestructibility. By the summer, he was back on top, and back on form. The show would go on. Instead of the RSC, it would be championed by another British cultural institution: the National Youth Theatre. Reunited at a party by Elton John's redoubtable manager John Reid (a tireless and faultlessly generous Chairman of the NYT) Bart and NYT director Ed Wilson decided on the show's viability for a cast of untried young enthusiasts. Lionel admired Wilson's spontaneity and decisiveness. Wilson, in turn, liked Bart's 'unique, child's-eye view of the period and its depiction of the irrepressible humour and determination of the community'. The author took his seat at rehearsals, occasionally making his presence felt. The £30,000 production opened for a limited run of twelve days at the Playhouse Theatre (then owned by Jeffrey Archer) on Monday 10 September 1990. Those who reviewed it were expectedly generous to its amateur cast, though less inclined to flatter the original work. In the *Evening Standard*, Annalena McAfee admonished those with resurrection mania. 'As with all revivals, the question must be asked whether it would be fairer to opt for non-interventionist euthanasia and let the subject rest in peace.' The *Daily Express* review commented that 'the show is so keen to evoke the warmth of working-class life that it gives the impression we fought a war in order to make the world safe for jellied eels.'

The Youth Theatre became an important champion, as well as pro-viding companionship, for Lionel and his work. Lionel enjoyed the hero-worhip. The NYT enjoyed the publicity from their association with the most esteemed talent they had been able to nurture since Peter Terson gave them *Zigger Zagger*. For their summer season of 1992, the same creative team of Ed Wilson and designer Brian Lee triumphed with a full-scale revival of the Liverpool dock epic *Maggie May* at the Royalty Theatre, London, at the beginning of September. After the first night performance, cast and audience met at a party, held on board a pleasure steamer moored on the Thames Embankment, where Lionel lapped up the admiration of his young team. By now, he had other reasons to be cheerful. He had decided to work on a dramatization of his life story – 'but it will take me a long time'. He was being fêted and honoured, though he tended to view it as 'being wheeled out to receive awards for being alive'. He had been asked by the impresario Duncan Weldon to write some material for a children's show by Adrian Mitchell. He was dreaming of a new fantasy musical about the homeless who had created Cardboard City beneath the Festival Hall. His first breakthrough song 'Rock With the Caveman' was to be recorded by Big Audio Dynamite for the soundtrack to the movie version of *The Flintstones*. He was fired up by Peggy Lee's success in suing Disney over video and CD rights that were owing to her, and began to send reams of faxes to lawyers in London and America in anticipation of a legal challenge that would have outlasted Jarndyce versus Jarndyce. He made a momentary return to the stage in *Consider Yourself!* – a 'side-by-side' musical celebrating his work, performed in Brighton to raise money for people with HIV and AIDS.[13] And, far more importantly, he was aware that a major revival of *Oliver!* was being discussed.

For some years Lionel had not sought to hide his festering resentment of those who had power over his past creative works. While he accepted responsibility for his irresponsibility in signing away his birthright, he still felt aggrieved at what it had taken from him and what it had driven him to. 'It came to a point where so many people laid claim to what I was doing. One publisher said, "Anything you write, even if you just think it, we own it before you do." There wasn't really much incentive to have an idea. I just went out and got drunk.' Bart also made frequent references to the stranglehold maintained on London theatres and particularly on musical revivals by Andrew Lloyd Webber and Cameron Mackintosh. And, as Bart was repeatedly making everyone aware, Cameron, who as a young stagehand had swept the set of *Oliver!*, had once – maybe twenty-five years ago – cheekily told Mr Bart that he would one day be presenting his own revival of the show. 'He did acquire the rights, and it helped set him up. I see Cameron now and again, but I don't think he quite believes that I am ready to work. And I don't really feel like having to prove it.' Not only that, Lionel was unhappy that Cameron was talking about a revival as part of his sponsorship of revivals from the classic musical repertoire at the National Theatre, and equally unhappy that Simon Russell Beale was being talked about as the next Fagin. Cameron, in turn, expressed his frustrations over Lionel: 'He was truly the Halley's Comet of the sixties, but comets do burn out a bit. I think his creative brain is still there.'

Without warning, full-page, full-colour advertisements appeared in newspapers. To anyone in the theatrical business, the icon of Fagin's battered hat with the L of Oliver forming an oversized proboscis, was the work of publicists Dewynters.[14] The show was destined to be a box-office-guaranteed, oversubscribed, technically unsurpassed, fully hyped monster. Almost as quickly, Jonathan Pryce was cast as Fagin, a role almost replicated in his wily Engineer for *Miss Saigon*. By February 1994, still more than ten months away from opening night, the Palladium had sold over £1 million worth of tickets; *The South Bank Show*[15] was planning to devote an edition to Lionel and the revival; the director appointed by Mackintosh was known to be Sam Mendes, still a relative newcomer; and speculation was being fuelled in showbusiness gossip columns about casting for Nancy. Would it be Ruthie Henshall (recently linked with Prince Edward), Linzi Hateley (who shone through the gore of *Carrie*), Sally Dexter[16] (from the National's production of *A Beggar's Opera*), or *EastEnders* landlady Letitia Dean? And as if in flashback to 1960, press photographers were welcomed to open auditions where stage-struck parents pushed forward 1,500 startled lads to warble 'I'd Do Anything'. The press was less welcome when it printed stories about thirty London schools which had been banned from going ahead with their stagings of the musical because of the imminence of a major West End revival. But in a change of heart worthy of another Dickensian hero, Cameron relented, allowing a restricted number of amateur performances to be run before the end of the year. Then, as a less welcome reminder of that first production, it was announced that Cameron's £3.5 million production had had its opening night put back three weeks, to 8 December 1994. The reason cited was 'the sheer scale of the production'. Mendes, however, played down any notion of overblown extravagance: 'It will have much the biggest stage I've ever worked on, the longest run, the biggest cast. But...I can guarantee that there won't be any braces twanging and there won't be any blowing the froth off tankards of beer.'

Slowly, another story was emerging. One which gladdened even the steel hearts in the entertainment industry. It became public knowledge that, in recognition of his boyhood hero and the importance to him of the genius behind *Oliver!*, Cameron had devised a scheme whereby Bart would receive a royalty from the production, by being given back a portion of the stage rights.[17] Better still, the author had been invited to rework parts of the show, since Cameron felt it unwise to ignore the impact the film version would have had on today's audiences, arriving at the theatre expecting lavish set pieces of design and choreography with costermongers cartwheeling around Covent Garden, and Nash Terraces reverberating to fanfares of flower-sellers. 'I am very involved in the production. I am not just being wheeled in for the first night. I am rescoring bits of it, I am adding to it, extending it. I am having a field day.'

It was entirely and undeniably Lionel's due. The fear of all artists is that their work will be taken from them, that their creativity will be denied them, that their glory will be snatched by another. For two decades Lionel Bart had looked on impotently as others traded and bartered his intellectual property. At last he would enjoy some financial security in his remaining years. There would be no need for further comebacks. He would not disappear from view again. 'This is not a sad story. I have been privileged. I sometimes feel as though I'm a historical figure. But the thing is I'm not history. I *am*. I'm here. I'm not dead, I'm alive. And I've earned the right to fail.'

NOTES

CHAPTER ONE

1. On Lionel's birth certificate, the address appears as Underwood Street. However, because the only Underwood Street is in Islington, it seems reasonable to assume that a mistake has been made by the registrar. Underwood Road is located a few hundred yards from Lionel's parental home.
2. Lionel's father's name is spelled variously over the years as Morris (on Lionel's birth certificate) or Maurice.
3. See Arthur Marwick's *Britain in the Century of Total War* (1968).
4. Entry for 2–7 February 1951, p. 16, from *The Kenneth Williams Diaries*, edited by Russell Davies (1993).
5. A corruption of *parlare*, brought to the public's ear by Kenneth Williams and Hugh Paddick in expressions such as 'varda that eek', 'bona lallies', 'polone', etc.
6. Professionally known as Danny La Rue, born in Cork, Ireland, on 26 July 1927 and raised in Soho, London.
7. Bart reported for duty at Padgate, near Warrington; his square-bashing was done at Credon Hill, Hereford; the rest of his National Service was carried out at RAF Innsworth, on the outskirts of Gloucester.
8. Apart from Renee, Bart has one other surviving sister and one surviving brother.
9. John Gold went on to work as a journalist for the *Financial Times*. He is married to the Unity actress Una Brandon-Jones. His brother Danny Gold is married to Bart's sister Renee – they also met at the IYC.

10. A much-loved English character actor, often cast as a loser, who became a household name thanks to the television series *Bootsie and Snudge*.

11. Later Lord Willis, who made his name as the creator of BBC Television's long-running *Dixon of Dock Green*.

12. The author of *England, Half English* and *Absolute Beginners* also gave Lionel some of his books 'with little love notes in the front'.

13. *Begleiter* is a German word meaning companion.

Chapter Two

1. Who later had a more lasting taste of fame in the 1969–70 television series *Randall & Hopkirk (Deceased)*. Michael John Pratt was born in London on 7 June 1931, and was described as having 'the weather-beaten looks of a mountainside which has been battered by the elements'. He died of lung cancer on 10 July 1976 at the age of forty-five.

2. The legendary music impresario was known by the unkind sobriquet Mr Parnes-Shillings-and-Pence.

3. A plaque now marks the site of the birth of rock 'n' roll at 59 Old Compton Street. The 2 I's was so named after its original owners, the Irani brothers, who sold the premises on in 1956 to two wrestlers from Australia, Ray Hunter and Paul Lincoln. Handling bookings for acts in the cellar club was a former stunt actor Tom Littlewood. Curiously, Bart's first published song is thought to be 'Oh for a Cup of Tea', written for the bandleader Billy Cotton. The lyric sends up the fashion for espresso bars.

4. For permission to quote this anecdote, the author is grateful to Steve Turner, in whose biography *Cliff Richard* (1993, 1994) it originally appears.

5. Released in the USA as *Rock Around the World*.

6. Better known as, respectively, director and producer of the *Carry On* films.

7. Released in the USA as *A Touch of Hell*.

8. The Drifters had their first two-week residency at the 2 I's in April 1958.

9. Jess continues his career in musical theatre, and in Steve Turner's definitive biography of Cliff Richard (op. cit.) recalls a visit made by Tommy Steele to the set of *Serious Charge*. 'There wasn't friction, but Tommy was the established star and now this new boy was coming up, and he asked Cliff if he had ever played knuckles, where you had to touch knuckles and if you couldn't move away fast enough you got hit. Tommy was very good at it and very fast. He cut Cliff's hands to ribbons. I'll never forget it. It was the most devious thing I had ever seen because Tommy had decided that he wanted to draw blood from the new idol. It was really awful. Cliff could never get out of the way quick enough and it went on and on. Cliff kept saying he'd play on, and yet his knuckles were red raw where Tommy had been whacking and whacking him.'

CHAPTER THREE

1. In *Theatrical Anecdotes* (Virgin, 1991), one of his many collections of apocrypha.

2. This was the third Mermaid Theatre – the first, built on Elizabethan lines in 1951, had been in a hall attached to the Mileses' house in St John's Wood, while the second was erected in the City in 1953 to celebrate the coronation of Elizabeth II.

3. 'Looks good, tastes good and, by golly, it does you good' was the slogan for long associated with Bernard Miles, who lent his talents to a number of other advertising campaigns, including the promotion of eggs stamped with a blue lion insignia to denote freshness. Far from sounding Cockney, he always seemed just to have stepped down from a hay-cart in Somerset.

4. Other, similar groups had been formed before the war, variously known as Theatre Action and Theatre Union, and these were clearly the antecedents of Theatre Workshop.

5. Lewenstein, along with George Devine, was responsible for the Royal Court Theatre.

6. As recalled in her peculiarly selective memoir, *Joan's Book* (Methuen, 1994).

7. Brendan Behan's play had opened at Stratford on 14 October 1958 for an eight-week run.

8. Co-produced by Oscar Lewenstein and Donald Albery. It opened in the West End on 10 February 1959, and ran at the Wyndham's and the Criterion for almost a year.

9. 'G'night Dearie' had been heard in the amateur production of *Wally Pone*.

10. The fashion for more rugged subjects in drama is still generally held to have originated in Osborne's 1956 state-of-nation play *Look Back in Anger*.

11. Miriam Karlin has since revised her opinion of the dominatrix. In an interview in 1994, she admitted: 'She's said some terrible things about me. That's what's so strange. You love the woman, and yet you can't bloody well trust her.'

12. *Cinderella* opened at the Coliseum on 18 December 1958.

13. *West Side Story* opened at Her Majesty's on 17 December 1958.

14. *Expresso Bongo* opened on 23 April 1958.

15. The London Academy of Music and Dramatic Art.

16. Eternally associated with Bernard Miles and the Mermaid.

CHAPTER FOUR

1. Lionel's memory almost serves him accurately: the plain chocolate bar was called 'Oliver Twist', and had a multi-coloured wrapper with a design featuring the orphan and his empty bowl. There was also a boxed version, containing plain chocolate drops. Both were manufactured by Terry's of York.

2. Although other reports have the figure as £350, it is understood that £1,000 was the figure settled upon, since it was the precise amount required by Bart to complete the production budget, enabling the show to go into rehearsal.

3. As late as 1960, the *Wimbledon Borough News* was reporting on Lionel Hart.

4. Originally, it was to have premièred at Lionel's alma mater, the Theatre Royal at Stratford East, but was previewed in Wimbledon when Stratford's stage proved too small to house Sean Kenny's immense sets.

5. The *Record Mirror* review of the London opening heaps praise upon the future housewife superstar: 'Barry Humphries has his moments as Mr Sowerberry, the Undertaker, and it is a pity, too, that this fine actor is offered no further opportunity than his splendidly performed song and dialogue sequence in the first act.'

6. Among Kretzmer's many credits are the lyrics to Charles Aznavour's hit 'She', as well as the English lyrics for *Les Misérables,* which had originally been attempted by the poet and theatre critic James Fenton.

7. A frothy confection by Julian Slade and Dorothy Reynolds. Despite mixed notices, it ran for 211 performances.

8. Lionel's Unity Theatre friend Jack Grossman commented: 'Some of the work from Unity turned up again in Lionel's shows. He jokingly admitted that he'd pinched a song from *Turn It Up* called "Be a Man, John Bull", which was recycled in *Oliver!* as "Be Back Soon" – but what the hell. What is an original tune?'

CHAPTER FIVE

1. Lionel Bart and Judy Garland were frequently romantically linked in the public perception. According to Leslie Bricusse, it was a true, deep friendship.

2. Bart was later to present the same gift, with the same dedication, to Caryl Brahms.

3. Cole Lesley was Coward's lifelong companion.

4. Michael Codron is still one of the more adventurous producers of serious drama.

5. According to some reports, the cast included the newcomers Terence Stamp and Michael Caine.

6. The John Barry Seven were responsible for the theme tune of the popular television series *Juke Box Jury*. John Barry has since emerged as a leading composer of film music.

7. Ralph Vaughan Williams collected traditional English folk songs.

8. See note 3 to Chapter Four.

9. At the time, reviews in the paper were still unsigned. This may have been the work of Ned Sherrin.

10. The case appears to have been settled out of court.

11. That same year Vivien Leigh was best female musical star in *Tovarich*; Beyond the Fringe was honoured for 'brilliance which has shattered all of the old

conceptions of comedy'; Anna Quayle was best supporting actress in a
musical – *Stop the World, I Want to Get Off*; best musical was Sondheim's *A
Funny Thing Happened on the Way to the Forum*; and best play was *Who's Afraid
of Virginia Woolf?*

12. Oliver Promotions is also the name of the company which currently owns
the rights to *Oliver!*

13. The film was released as *Sparrows Can't Sing*.

14. Other sources claim, with equal authority, that Oldham's mother was acting
as legal guardian.

15. Bryan had produced the film *The Horse's Mouth* and had also designed the sets
for *Becket* – which were to furnish Bart's new home. He was down to provide
the stage sets for what was then known as *Robin Hood*.

CHAPTER SIX

1. The American dramatist, who wrote the original book of *Twang!!* with Bart,
had at one time been a scriptwriter for the Marx Brothers.

2. The respected Canadian choreographer had been described by Lionel as 'on a
par with Jerome Robbins'. Miss Littlewood is on record as saying: 'Paddy
Stone was a bum.'

3. Who played Little John.

4. On 4 October 1978 *Jesus Christ Superstar* became the longest-running
theatrical show in British history. It had played 2,620 performances, beating
the previous record held by *Oliver!*

5. In a letter published in the *Guardian* on 17 January 1966.

6. One of Bart's frequently retold stories is that the original lyric was
'Scrambled Eggs', and that he suggested the change to what is now an
immortal song. However, in her biography *Alma Cogan – A Memoir*, the
author, Alma's sister Sandra Caron, has a clear recollection (see pp. 160–61)
of Paul McCartney composing the song late one night in Alma's mother's
Kensington apartment, with no sign of Lionel. In all other respects, the
anecdote is identical.

7. Spinetti was an actor with Theatre Workshop, and became a friend of the
Beatles. He now performs a one-man show of his priceless theatrical anecdotes.

8. In fact Bart's recorded music (whether composed solo or collaboratively)
totals 248 compositions. See Discography, pp. 175–9.

9. Described by one critic as 'tasteless nonsense about four screwy London
mods who kidnap a popular singing idol to satisfy their sexual appetites.
Should be seen with a deodorizer handy, if you must.'

CHAPTER SEVEN

1. *Daily Telegraph*, 4 June 1964.

2. *Daily Telegraph*, 17 April 1964.

3. Producers of the stage version of the musical.

4. Curiously, Sellers resigned his directorship of Brookfield in April 1964.

5. The actual sum offered, on 5 May 1964, was $400,000.

6. This effectively meant Montpelier Arts and Enterprises Ltd, the theatrical agents who handled most of Bart's business affairs, Oliver Promotions Ltd and Lionel Bart Ltd.

7. $450,000.

8. $112,500.

9. $100,000.

10. Who had already played a sinister Fagin in David Lean's film *Oliver Twist*.

11. Lester is now an osteopath in Cheltenham. His career continued immediately after *Oliver!* with *Run Wild, Run Free*, and later *Black Beauty*. He worked for a second time with Jack Wild on the flop *Melody*. His name for many years made regular appearances in the tabloids after he inherited the fortune earned from childhood acting.

12. Wild is today trying to complete an animated film about cats. His adult career has not been distinguished.

CHAPTER EIGHT

1. Who had published most of the Bart–Pratt–Steele compositions.

2. A 1973 pirate adventure, which coincidentally co-starred Mark Lester. Douglas is an unlikely bearded peg-leg buccaneer, and he also directed. It is not known whether Lionel's music was used in the final cut.

3. If Mark Steyn's retelling of the anecdote is to be believed, on one of these Caribbean vacations at Princess Margaret's villa on Mustique, Lionel staggered down bleary-eyed one morning to find her poring over various figures. 'What you doin'?' he asked. 'I'm doing my books,' said the Princess. 'If you'd done yours, you wouldn't be in the state you're in now.'

4. At other times he says she was forty-six.

5. See note 2 to Chapter Four.

CHAPTER NINE

1. Among them is Julian Jones, son of the Rolling Stone Brian Jones. Julian's stepfather is the singer Donovan. For several years after Jones's unexplained death in his own swimming pool, Bart kept the guitarist's sheepskin coat on a peg in the hall of his Reece Mews flat.

2. According to Lionel, his exact words were: 'I suppose I'm a Commie, homo junkie'.

3. Undoubtedly Bart is referring to Alma Cogan, who once publicly proposed marriage to him during the television programme *This Is Your Life* hosted by Eamonn Andrews. Alma, the girl with the laugh in her voice, died of cancer on 26 October 1966 at the age of thirty-four.

4. Who went on to invent pyramid selling.

5. Perhaps better known as a society photographer.

6. Recently better known in his role as Mark Fowler in BBC Television's *EastEnders*.

7. See note 7 to Chapter Six.

8. Lionel was, in fact, at the Tyne Theatre and Opera House in Newcastle to watch Bill Kenwright's production of *Blitz!* starring Diane Langton.

9. In his book *The Dynamics of Creation* (1972).

10. Although Bricusse is best known for his partnership with Anthony Newley, he did in fact write two songs with Bart, one of which – 'The Rhythm of the World' – was a success for Ray Ellington, a sometime wrestler who was known as 'the body beautiful of British show business'.

11. Alma and her mother were renowned for these 'all-nighters' which attracted the cream of local and visiting show people. A buffet supper was provided for cabaret artistes to let their hair down after a performance at, say, the Talk of the Town. The guest list in the early sixties often included the Beatles, Judy Garland, Sammy Davis, and so on.

12. Featuring, incidentally, Barbra Streisand, whose name was again quickly associated with this project, then just as quickly dropped because of her flat refusal ever to take to the stage again after a PLO death threat during her Central Park concert.

13. Author of, among other works, *Two for the See-Saw* and *The Miracle Worker*.

CHAPTER TEN

1. Which, as the New Theatre, had been its original home. This particular revival was presented by Cameron Mackintosh, but despite a successful tour the management found it necessary to offer free seats to children accompanying a paying adult. Lionel's 'consultation fee' was established during the first run, and continued to be paid during the second London revival at the Aldwych. The fee was agreed by Derek Dawson who, at the time, completely owned the stage rights.

2. Friendly strangers, however – Bart's flat belonged to Adam Faith and later to Leo Sayer.

3. Lionel continues to believe that he and Johnny Speight were born in the same street in the same week. In fact, Mr Speight was born over ten years earlier, on 2 June 1920, in Canning Town.

4. A production starring Adam Faith and Anita Dobson did eventually open at the Cambridge Theatre in 1988, to very little acclaim. The lyrics were by Don Black.

5. John Barton, Victor Spinetti and Susannah Fellows.

6. On 21 May 1988.

7. Peter and Iona Opie were a husband and wife team dedicated to collecting nursery rhymes and traditional children's songs.

8. Although the advertisement used the lyric and title 'Abbey Endings', for commercial reasons the single was released as 'Happy Endings'.

9. One report puts the price at £8 million, though this seems a shade inflated, even in the Thatcherite boom economy of 1988–9.

10. Creator of the classic camp musical *The Rocky Horror Show*, and sometime presenter of Channel 4's *The Crystal Maze*.

11. BBC Television's arts documentary strand.

12. The present author.

13. In July and August 1981 Bart was reported by the tabloid press to be 'desperately fighting a secret illness'. Commenting on Bart's two-month stay in St Mary's Hospital, Paddington, the article hinted at a terminal disease: 'Friends who have visited him have been alarmed at his dramatic weight loss. For three weeks he has been in a private room on a ward for serious heart-cases.' When eventually he recovered, Bart revealed that he had been suffering from a pulmonary congestion.

14. Also responsible for the *Cats* eye logo, the *Phantom* mask, the *Misérables* waif and more.

15. London Weekend Television's sempiternal arts documentary strand, edited and fronted by Melvyn Bragg.

16. Eventually chosen to play Nancy.

17. The rights to *Oliver!* are still divided among a complicated network of companies and subsidiaries. The Grand Rights in Perpetuity (those needed to perform the music in a dramatic fashion) are held by Oliver Promotions. This company belongs to Cameron Mackintosh (50 per cent, purchased in 1994) and to the Southbrook Group (50 per cent). The Southbrook Group is headed by Derek Dawson, who purchased Lionel's rights in the 1960s. The Professional Rights (those needed for stock or other performances) are owned by Oliver Productions. This company also belongs to Cameron Mackintosh (50 per cent) and the Southbrook Group (50 per cent). Since 1994 Cameron Mackintosh also owns shares in Southbrook Group, which has bought out most of the companies owning parts of *Oliver!* However, there are still a number of parties entitled to a share of profits, and they continue to receive these.

   Lionel Bart today receives a royalty for the work he has provided in rewriting parts of the score. He also receives an additional royalty, generously offered by Cameron Mackintosh in recognition of his previous creative contribution.

   Bart himself is a director of only one limited company, Bart Music Ltd, founded in 1986. John Gorman is company secretary. The company appears to be dormant, with no history of ever having traded. Latest accounts show only £100 cash in hand.

SHOWS

Shows for which Lionel Bart has composed at least one song or theme, or in which he appears. Only original opening dates (where known) are given; transfers have not been included.

The Wages of Eve (exact contribution unclear): Unity Theatre, 1953
Turn It Up: Unity Theatre, June 1953
Cinderella: Unity Theatre, December 1953
Wally Pone, King of the Underworld: Unity Theatre, 18 July 1958
Fings Ain't Wot They Used t'Be: Theatre Royal, Stratford East, 17 February 1959
Lock Up Your Daughters: Mermaid Theatre, 28 May 1959
Oliver!: New (Albery) Theatre, 30 June 1960
Blitz!: Adelphi Theatre, 8 May 1962
Maggie May: Adelphi Theatre, 22 September 1964
Twang!!: Shaftesbury Theatre, 20 December,1965
La Strada: Lunt-Fontanne Theatre, 14 December 1969
The Londoners: Theatre Royal, Stratford East, 27 March 1972
Costa Packet: Theatre Royal, Stratford East, 5 October 1972
Lionel: New London Theatre, 16 May 1977
Winnie: Victoria Palace Theatre, 21 May 1988
Consider Yourself!: Brighton Cares AIDS Benefit, 18 January 1992

FILMOGRAPHY

Films for which Lionel Bart has composed at least one song or theme, or in which he appears.

The Tommy Steele Story (1957)
The Duke Wore Jeans (1958)
Serious Charge (1959)
In the Nick (1959)
Heart of a Man (1959)
Tommy the Toreador (1959)
Let's Get Married (1960)
Light Up the Sky (1960)
From Russia With Love (1963)
Sparrows Can't Sing (1963)
Man in the Middle (1964)
Oliver! (1968)
The Touchables (1968)
Lock Up Your Daughters (1969)
Black Beauty (1971)
Scalawag (1973)
The Optimists (of Nine Elms) (1973)
The Alternative Miss World★ (1980)

★Lionel was a judge, along with Joan Bakewell and Michael Fish.

Currently registered recordings by Lionel Bart. This discography does not include deletions, and is not a comprehensive list of compositions.

Abracadabra
All My Worldly Possessions
All's Well (with Laurie Johnson)
Altogether Now
Always You and Me (with Trevor H Stanford)
Amanda (with Michael Pratt and Tommy Steele)
An American Lady (with Roger Cook)
Amsterdam
Another Morning
Ask a Silly Question (with Herbie Flowers and B A Robertson)
As Long As He Needs Me
As Long As This Is England
Away From Home
Bake a Cake
The Ballad of the Liver Birds
Be Back Soon
Be What You Wanna Be
Big Time
Black Beauty
Blitz/Who Wants to Settle Down/ Cry on the Streets
Bond Meets Tania (with John Barry)
Bonnie Prince Charlie (with Charles Rogers)
Boy for Sale
Build Up (with Michael Pratt and Tommy Steele)
Butterfingers (with Michael Pratt and Tommy Steele)

Cannibal Pot (with Michael Pratt and Tommy Steele)
Carryin' On
Carve Up
Casey
The Ceilin's Coming Dahn, The Ceilin's Coming Dahn
Choose
Cochran Will Return
Consider Yourself
Contempery
Cop a Bit of Pride
Danger Route
The Day After Tomorrow
Death of Kerim (with John Barry)
Dey Don't Do Dhat Today
The Ding Dong Song/The Second Spring (with Ming Tao)
Doomsday Rock/Kellner Rock (with Michael Pratt and Tommy Steele)
Down the Lane
Do You Mind?
Dreamchild
D'Same Size Boots
Duty Calls
Easter Bells (with Roger Cook)
Easy-Going Me
Entr'acte
Eskimoses (with Michael Pratt and Tommy Steele)
Family Tree (with Michael Pratt and Tommy Steele)
Fanciful Gal
Fanfare
Far Away
Fiesta (with Jimmy Bennett and Michael Pratt)
Fings Ain't Wot They Used t'Be

Follow Your Leader

Food, Glorious Food

For the Love of Mike

From Off the Top of Her Head (with Roger Cook)

From One Tree (with Roger Cook)

From Russia With Love

Gangin' Hame

The Gentle Art of Seduction (with Laurie Johnson)

Getting It Together

Girl Trouble (with John Barry)

Give Us a Kiss for Christmas

Goodbye-Mommy-and-Daddy-Day

Goodbye Morning Tokyo/Tokyo Melody (with Monique Falk and Helmut Zacharias)

Goodnight Dearie/G'Night Dearie

Grandad's Rock (with Una Bart and Tommy Steele)

Gypsy Camp (with John Barry)

Hair-Down Hoe-Down (with Michael Pratt and Tommy Steele)

A Handful of Songs (with Michael Pratt and Tommy Steele)

Happiness

Happy Endings (Give Yourself a Pinch/Give Yourself a Pinch Party)

Happy Guitar (with Michael Pratt and Tommy Steele)

Heatha an' Haggis an' Sporran

Hey You (with Tommy Steele)

Hide and Seek

His Kiss

I Aim at the Stars (with Laurie Johnson)

I'd Do Anything

If He's Bare Under There

If I'd Known You/If I Knew You (with Laurie Johnson)

If Only I Were Made of Stone

I Got a Pailful of Milk (with Michael Pratt and Tommy Steele)

I Like (with Michael Pratt and Tommy Steele)

I'll Be Hanged

I'll Be There (with Laurie Johnson)

I Love a Man

The I Love You Bit

I'm Me

In the Movies

In the Nick

Introduction

I Puts the Lightie On (with Tommy Steele)

I Seen You (with Michael Pratt)

I Shall Scream

Is This Gonna Be a Wedding

It Goes to Show (with Roger Cook)

I Thought I Knew Why (with Roger Cook)

It Must Be True (with Laurie Johnson)

I Told You So

It's a Definite Maybe (with Roger Cook)

It's a Fine Life

It's All Happening (with Michael Pratt and Tommy Steele)

It's Hard

It's Yourself/It's Yourself I Love

I Want to Whisper Something

James Bond With Bongos (with John Barry)

Jellied Eels

Julie the Redhead/Julie la Rousse (with René Louis Lafforgue)

Just to While Away the Night

Kickin' Up the Leaves

Kind Fate (with Laurie Johnson)

The Land of Promises

Layin' Abaht

Leave Her, Johnny, Leave Her

Leave It to the Ladies

Leila Dances/Laila Dances (with John Barry)

Let's Get Married

Let's Start All Over

Light Up the Sky

Little Boy Blue

Little Cutie

Little White Bull (with Jimmy Bennett and Michael Pratt)

Living Doll

Living in Dreamland

Living Love (with Maggie Swanepoel)

Lock Up Your Daughters (with Laurie Johnson)

Looking Glass, Looking Glass

Lovely Lover (with Laurie Johnson)

Mad About You

Maggie May

Make an Honest Woman of Me

The March of the Women (with Roger Cook)

May a Man Be Merry

Meat Face

Meeting in St Sophia (with John Barry)

Milwaukee (with Roger Cook)

Morris Dance

Mr Jones/Mister Jones (with Laurie Johnson)

Mums and Dads

Must Be/This Must Be the Place

My Name

Neon Sign (with Tommy Steele)

Next Year in Jerusalem (with Roger Cook)

Across the Way/Number Twenty-Two Across the Way (with Tommy Steele)

Nobody in Particular (with Roger Cook)

No More (from *Man in the Middle*)

No Turning Back

Och an' Aye

Oh My My My (with Roger Cook)

Oliver/Finale from *Oliver!*

On a Sunny Sunday Morning (with Laurie Johnson)

One Potato, Two Potato (with Roger Cook)

On the Side (with Laurie Johnson)

Oom-Pah-Pah

Opposites

Our Hotel

Over and Over

Overture

Part Two the Child

Petticoat Lane

Photograph (with Michael Pratt and Tommy Steele)

Place in the Old Country

Plant a Kiss (with Tommy Steele)

Polka Dots

Pretty Daisy (with Michael Pratt and Tommy Steele)

Princess (with Michael Pratt and Tommy Steele)

A Proper Man (with Laurie Johnson)

Quasimodo

Red Wine (with Laurie Johnson)

Red Wine and a Wench (with Laurie Johnson)

Reviewing the Situation/I'm Reviewing the Situation

Right of Way

Rock With the Caveman (with Frank Chacksfield, Michael Pratt and Tommy Steele)

Roger the Ugly

The Royal Smile

School's Out

Selection from *Oliver!*

Sex

Shine, You Swine/Shine, You Swine Sunshine You

177

Sighs

Singing Time (with Jimmy Bennett and Michael Pratt)

Sketch Blumas (with Roger Cook)

Something Special

Sometimes

Sometime Somewhere (with Frankie Vaughan)

Sorry But That's Where...

So Tell Me

Sparrers Can't Sing

Spoilsport (with Michael Pratt)

Stalking (with John Barry)

La Strada

Stroll On

The Student Ponce

Sunday Sunday Morning (with Laurie Johnson)

Take a Ride (with Jimmy Bennett and Michael Pratt)

Take Me Back Baby (with Tommy Steele)

Talk Proper (with Michael Pratt)

Tania Meets Klebb (with John Barry)

Tattle Tale (with Roger Cook)

Tell Him, Tell Her

Thanks a Lot (with Michael Pratt and Tommy Steele)

That's Your Funeral

There's a Plot Afoot (with Laurie Johnson)

There's Only One Union

Throwaway Collapsible Soapbox

Till the Day That I Die (with John Cameron)

Time to Kill (with Michael Pratt and Tommy Steele)

'Tis Plain to See (with Laurie Johnson)

To Be a Performer

Tommy the Toreador (with Jimmy Bennett and Tommy Steele)

Too Much of a Good Thing

Too Young for Sad Memories

To the Woods

Twang

Two Eyes (with Michael Pratt and Tommy Steele)

Unseen Hands

Waarheen Vliegen De Voge

Wander

Water Water (with Michael Pratt and Tommy Steele)

The Way It's Meant to Be (with Herbie Flowers and B A Robertson)

We Don't All Wear D'Same Size Boots

Welcome to Sherwood

We'll Live (with Roger Cook)

We're Going to the Country

We Will Never Be As Young Again (with Trevor H. Stanford)

What Do You Do? (with Jimmy Bennett, Michael Pratt and Tommy Steele)

What Makes a Star?

When Does the Ravishing Begin? (with Laurie Johnson)

Where Do Little Birds Go?

Where Is Love?

Where It's Hot

Where's the Birdie? (with Jimmy Bennett and Michael Pratt)

Whose Little Girl Are You?

Who's This Geezer Hitler?

Who Will Buy?

Wild Cat (with Marty Wilde)

Will It Be You? (with Michael Pratt and Tommy Steele)

Winnie

With Bells On

The World's a Lovely Place

You Can't Catch Me

You Gotta Go (with Michael Pratt and Tommy Steele)

The Young Ones and Living Doll

(with Richard Curtis, Ade
Edmondson, Ben Elton, Rik
Mayall, Lisa Mayer, Nigel Planer
and Christopher Ryan)
You've Got to Pick a Pocket/Pick a
Pocket or Two